Human Nature against Socialism

Human Nature against Socialism

Germinal Boloix

Germinal Boloix
2019

Copyright © 2019 by Germinal Boloix
All rights reserved. This book or any portion thereof may not be reproduced or used in any manner whatsoever without the express written permission of the author except for the use of brief quotations in a book review or scholarly journal.

Front Cover: "Diversity and Imperfection"

First Printing: 2019

ISBN 978-0-9958612-9-9

Germinal Boloix
email: gboloix@hotmail.com
Blog: gboloix.blogspot.com

Dedication

To all Venezuelans confronting Absurd Socialism.

Contents

Germinal Boloix 3
Acknowledgments 9
Preface 11
Introduction 15
Part I: Background 27
Chapter 1: Socialism and Reality 29
Chapter 2: Human Evolution 40
Chapter 3: Social Groupings 48
Chapter 4: Human Values 56
Part II: Behavioral Framework 65
Chapter 5: Life Motivators 67
Chapter 6: Doing or Acting 75
Chapter 7: Personal Influence 79
Chapter 8: Social Influence 86
Chapter 9: Justifications 90
Part III: Human Influence 95
Chapter 10: Human Happiness 97
Chapter 11: Attention and Memory 104
Chapter 12: Emotions 107
Chapter 13: Credulity 116
Chapter 14: Responsibility 124
Chapter 15: Reality versus Fantasy 129
Chapter 16: Egocentricity 134
Chapter 17: Judging 140
Chapter 18: Unusual Reactions 145
Part IV: Evaluating Socialism 153

Chapter 19: Motivations 155
Chapter 20: Actions 162
Chapter 21: Personal Factors 167
Chapter 21: Social Factors 173
Chapter 22: Rationale 177
Bibliography 183
Epilogue 185

Acknowledgments

I want to thank all the libraries and coffee shops that welcomed me during many hours of thinking, reading, and writing.

Preface

The world is diverse and imperfect, humans are different physically and mentally. It is difficult to manage human societies, everyone has a particular say on things. There is too much poverty, discrimination, and injustice that societies are not capable of coping with. Humans have been exploiting other fellow humans in one way or another and this is another source of nonconformity. The hope is to diminish suffering and exploitation offering better opportunities for living better to everybody.

One thing must be clear though, perfection is unattainable, it is too naive to think that a new political system is going to transform the world. Socialists are quite naive believing it is possible to transform the world upside down, they think today people are capitalists and tomorrow they will be sanctified socialists, No way Jose! It is not possible to change human beings, they are stubborn, they keep their originality independently of the political system. Therefore, political systems must obey human nature instead of the current view where people must obey the system.

The book identifies most human nature characteristics defining the behavior of humans and contrasting them with socialist beliefs. Socialists have exploited the understanding of some human's weaknesses but have failed to interpret them. Socialism imposition of a unique viewpoint that has to be accepted by everybody is a misunderstanding of human's idiosyncratic nature. A society must be run to handle diversity instead of uniformity, socialists fail because of their uniformity viewpoint.

Socialism is one stage before communism, as Marx properly stated, therefore, socialism should not be the objective of the lovers of freedom. There are several reasons why human nature opposes socialism, let us mention just a few of them: equality, authoritarianism, collectivization, freedom, and diversity. First, socialism proposes an undefined concept of equality among humans where good behavior and skills are underrated to transform people into equal zombies. Under these conditions, equality without restraint is borne to failure. Second, each experience of socialism has failed because of its authoritarian approach to stay in power. People have the right to a prosperous life and socialism represents misery. Third, socialism forces the population to accept a unique collectivization viewpoint where there is no possibility of individual initiative. Collectivization has been a fiasco every time it has been tried. Fourth, socialism limits the freedom of individuals and enterprises. Innovation is doomed under socialism. And finally, socialism does not consider the diversity of human beings. People cannot accept doctrines based on a unique viewpoint.

The title of the book says it all: Human Nature against Socialism, humans cannot tolerate a doctrine that goes against their innate humanity. Socialism has been a failure but it stays popular among those at the lower echelons of society. There have been several experiences demonstrating its non-viability but socialists still find supporters. It is a paradox that some people are still cheering for it independently of its inefficiency. It is understandable poor people see socialism as an alternative because they don't expect a better future under the current political system. They don't understand that constant effort is necessary to improve in life. Socialism is plenty of pitfalls, there is no valid reason to believe it is viable. Socialism is still there because Democrats have not been able to convince the poor. Socialists get support from the population because they exploit people's ignorance.

Socialism imposes a homogeneous view of the world that is opposed to human nature. Human nature is full of diversity, therefore, any political system must organize the population around that concept. Socialist's ideology does not demonstrate an understanding of humans; socialism promotes equality between humans without analyzing how humans behave; socialism promotes a fictive society unrelated to reality; socialism invents an unfair justice in favor of cheating and slacking.

Socialism has always been portrayed as the solution to all democracy and capitalism problems. Socialists criticize democracy and capitalism proposing a new society where people should not be egotistic and sharing all resources for the good of the people. The big mistake of socialism is not knowing how wealth is produced, socialists run against the private property and towards the supremacy of the state, thinking it is a good idea to run a centralized society. Socialists count with the support of part of the population that believes that work and effort are not necessary to progress in life.

It is important to point out that when socialism is used under the democratic umbrella, for example, social democracy, it is an acceptable approach even though with some weaknesses. Implementing measures that benefit the population and maintain the possibility of correcting mistakes is an acceptable perspective. Most democratic and capitalistic systems include benefits to the population, social programs have been available in most capitalistic countries. It is not only socialism the one suggesting welfare to the population.

Socialism becomes an autocracy because there is no other alternative when a unique anti-nature approach is imposed. In authoritarian socialistic regimes, the population has no say in public policy. Decisions are already taken by the party in power or the dictator in charge. Therefore, beware of socialism, it always takes the authoritarian highway. However, the population is smart enough to notice its failure. People know that things change for the worst under socialism but they cannot fight against the monster state. But that is changing with so many unsuccessful socialists experiences.

The main justification to write this book is the sufferings Absurd Socialism has inflicted in Venezuela, a small country in South America. No society deserves the fate Venezuela is going through. Socialists may say that the Venezuelan case is not the fault of socialism, that it was the wrongdoings of a lieutenant colonel or the negligence of a bus driver. I dismiss those explanations and assign responsibility to the political system imposed by the fanatics of socialism and communism. The book shows no mercy towards the socialist's ideology, even though it stands out its strong point, the control and submission of the population.

For this book, it is fundamental to point out the importance of human nature in political systems. These systems are made to serve a society that is composed of humans displaying random behavior. Additionally, every person must understand human nature to better relate to others. It is good news to recognize that human nature should be known by every citizen because it is fundamental to run a well-balanced society.

Describing the book in two words, they would be 'diversity' and 'imperfection.' In all the subjects being discussed in the book, diversity must be remembered. Human beings are different, they are not equal and they are imperfect, it is inconvenient to generalize. However, there is so much diversity that it is impossible to describe all the cases and organize society around those parameters. Therefore, the best that can be done in this book is to identify some important human characteristics and determine how socialism performs.

Introduction

"Image there's no heaven," "Imagine there's no countries," "Imagine all the people, Living life in peace, aha-ah ah ah ah" ... John Lennon.

Imagine is a beautiful song, I do like it. "You may say I'm a dreamer, but I'm not the only one." Many people are dreamers and there is nothing wrong with that, the problem is to confuse dreams with reality. To make a dream a reality, the first thing is to understand the world, then identify the feasible aspects of your dream, those that are beneficial, and implement them into the social reality. Not everything will be attainable in a realistic world, some improvements will be feasible while others will be omitted. The world is not perfect and there is no point in trying to create a perfect world. Let us live better even though with some imperfections. Socialism is a dream that has not performed a critical analysis of its feasibility. If socialism were a song, I'll be happy to sing it everyday but being an erroneous political approach I'm happy fighting every day against it with all my heart.

Most political systems forget to consider human nature in their approaches and choose to apply biased policies invented by bureaucrats. Humanism would be the only philosophy that considers the innate characteristics of humans but has not been portrayed as a political system. Modern political approaches require human nature considerations to design a doctrine oriented to humans. To succeed in attaining practical goals in a society, human nature must be in the center of all political approaches. Political systems tend to dismiss human nature characteristics in subjects such as ideology, society, culture, and economic frameworks. The search for an impossible new humanoid seems rooted deep down in socialist and communist ideals.

Let us make the analogy of society with cooking, where each group of ingredients represents similar types of people. A soup, for example, can be made of vegetables, meat, noodles, liquid, and species. Once the soup is cooked following the recipe, it can be served in a bowl where all the ingredients are visible and where each ingredient keeps its identity. However, the soup can be processed in a blender making it into a cream. Comparing both approaches in political terms, the original soup would be similar to democracy under a capital or social democracy economy and the cream would be similar to a socialist or communist economy. In the first approach, the differences within the society are maintained whilst in the second everybody gets crushed, the individual disappears. I like the soup in any form and I would eat it as it comes. However, in politics, I dislike a socialist system that insists on making people equal to an invented standard.

Any political system proposing a doctrine to stimulate humans as physically and intellectually equal is borne to failure. One distinctive characteristic of humans is diversity. People are different, even though they share common characteristics. Humans are different and they deserve their individuality; they have a mix of biological diversity, personality differences, and cultural idiosyncrasies. Different people can get together to complete great enterprises and everybody can collaborate to attain collective objectives without losing their individuality.

The individual is the main actor in life and groups are formed around several persons to attain objectives. A theory of the group must emphasize the individual. Groups can be many, not just one unique fictitious collective group, and each group is formed by different individuals. Each group must respect the principles of reasoning brought about by individuals and accepted within the groups. Groups must respect other groups, and groups don't have to be similar or follow the same pattern. Finally, the interaction among individuals and groups as well as their principles of reasoning are defined according to behavioral principles.

Societies are composed of individuals who join groups to serve communities and nations. Societies must incorporate human nature concepts in the definition of their structure, considering primarily diversity among individuals. Some groups may be productive just by incorporating homogeneous individuals whilst in other groups heterogeneity should be the norm.

Sociologists, psychologists, and psychiatrists are the most capable professionals that could fill the requirement to understand human nature. They can define the knowledge about human nature and identify which are the features distinguishing human beings. There is an extensive literature about human nature that provides a solid background on the characteristics of humans and their evolution. Trying to generalize results to explain human nature is very discouraging because most people are completely different. Additionally, there is a biological component that usually is not considered by these professions.

Human nature must be studied from many angles, incorporating new and diverse perspectives. Some amusing anecdotes, some feuds, and some mismatched results have created a weak foundation on the application of human nature concepts. Academics should consider their research to be the property of all humanity. Academics feel superior thinking they know more than others but they must accept the opinion of other experts. Academics should accept their ignorance. The integration of several areas of research requires more scientific rigor and application of human nature concepts in society.

The vast majority of research studies have been oriented towards solving specific mental problems to improve the lives of those affected. Most people we know, those that seem normal, may have some hidden disorder that can be treated using approaches already developed for severe maladies. Psychological disorders, complexes, and delusions found in nervous diseases are fundamentally no different in structure from the behavior of normal individuals. This is a favorable point to help understand human nature in general. [Adler 1992]

People's behavioral mechanisms are different. No two people have the same amount of aggressiveness or defensiveness in a specific scenario. Most people look for safety while others are capable of taking greater risks. In a society, individual objectives have to be considered, it is not convenient to equalize all humans. Psychological activity is a complex of behavioral mechanisms whose final purpose is to guarantee the continued existence of the organism and to enable it to develop in safety. [Adler 1992]

Socialists should understand human evolution and identify the important evolutionary milestones affecting the characteristics of humans. Humans are not recent creatures appearing on Earth, ancient humanoids were here millions of years ago. Socialism is a recent myth that has had difficulty to catch up, there are no successful experiences.

The following Timeline of History (Years Ago) would be a good starting point for socialists, the evolution has lasted millions of years, they should understand human nature better than they do. [Harari 2014]

- 2.5 million - Evolution of the genus Homo in Africa. First stone tools.
- 2 million - Humans spread from Africa to Eurasia. Evolution of different human species.
- 500,000 - Neanderthals evolved in Europe and the Middle East.

- 300,000 - Daily usage of fire.
- 200,000 - Homo sapiens evolved in East Africa.
- 70,000 - The Cognitive Revolution. The emergence of fiction and language. Beginning of history. Sapiens spread out of Africa.
- 45,000 - Sapiens settle Australia. Extinction of Australian megafauna.
- 30,000 - Extinction of Neanderthals.
- 16,000 - Sapiens settle in America. Extinction of American megafauna.
- 13,000 - Extinction of Homo floresiensis. Homo sapiens the only surviving human species.
- 12,000 - The Agricultural Revolution. Domestication of plants and animals. Permanent settlements.
- 500 - The Scientific Revolution.

The book is divided into four parts, Background, Human Influence, Behavioral Framework, and Evaluating Socialism. Part I, Background, includes issues of socialism and reality, human evolution, groupings, and human values.

Socialism and reality explain the relationship of socialism with reality. Humans have innate predispositions to certain types of social organizations and socialists have not been able to understand the complexity of human interactions. World improvement has been a common objective of most political systems. To improve the world people need to understand how it works, the tragedy of the commons is an example that introduces the difficulties of working for a common objective, and cheating and slacking are the result of human misunderstandings. There is a need for regulations to make a functional world; cooperation is not an automatic behavior in humans, it requires reinforcement. Cult culture has been a common approach pursued by humans for hundreds of thousands of years, popularized to make people participate and cooperate. Finally, the recent Venezuelan case is presented to confirm the failure of socialism under Absurd Socialism.

Human evolution presents some basic considerations about evolution. Both biological and cultural evolution have an impact on human behavior. Both types of evolution are important and that knowledge would help to devise political systems designed to serve every human and not just the socialist elite. The division of labor was one of the most important choices humans made to live a better life. The mind and the brain are discussed to understand the innate characteristics of humans that define their weaknesses in so many aspects. Language and knowledge are the instruments used by humans to live a better life.

Groupings present a summary of the risks and benefits of organizing people in groups. Groups are organized around imagined orders and communities which make them unstable. Group conformity, group inefficiency, and group limitations are group characteristics that must be taken into consideration to design political systems.

Human values are independent of political systems and any ideology must consider them. Several human values have been identified, humanism, equality, freedom, free will, and social justice. Human virtues, industriousness, optimism and pessimism, tolerance, and forgiveness complete the brief summary of human values.

Part II, Behavioral Framework, presents the structure to organize the characteristics of human behavior. The structure of the framework includes life motivators, doing or acting, personal influence, social influence, and justifications.

Life motivators are organized along with needs, beliefs, and desires. Maslow's hierarchy of needs is a good starting point to identify most human needs. It identifies physiological, safety, esteem, love and belonging, and self-actualization needs. Beliefs are mental representations or patterns our brain expects the world to conform to. They are templates for efficient learning and are often essential for survival. Desires are intimately connected to pleasure and pain and respond to many innate behaviors. Self-control helps us reduce the potential danger of consequences for our desires by a conscious learning and acting approach. Factors such as intentions, interests, illusions, and suffering are related to the individual and its surroundings.

Doing or acting is related to an active life. Only by welcoming sharp adversity will people ever begin to discover their mettle. The will to power, the will to love, the will to justice, the will to knowledge, are ways of stressing action, the need to be active instead of passive. It is oriented to be active, to take a position, to challenge old ideas, and so on.

Personal influence is related to individual characteristics. Persons are moral beings, conscious of right and wrong, who judge their fellows and who are judged in their turn. To be a person, therefore, people must have the capacities that make relationships possible. Personality is the unique, integrated and organized system of all behavior of a person. Personality indicators provide the characteristic ways people prefer to focus their attention, take in information, make decisions, and deal with the outer world. Human rights are principles that any political system must consider. Civil, political, social, economic, cultural and collective rights involve some considerations that any political system must contemplate.

Social influence is related to society's social issues. Humans are imperfect. Either biologically or culturally, humans are random organisms. Diversity is an appreciated concept. Humans have so many characteristics that their combinations can produce infinite types of variants. One characteristic that distinguishes humans is that we understand things differently. Obedience, respect and dignity, love and empathy, and altruism are other characteristics to build a prosperous society.

Justifications are explanations to support people's beliefs, actions, personal approaches or social decision making. But has people decreased the amount of suffering in the world? Humans have plenty of alternatives to choose from when deciding the course of their society, which by itself is a good thing. Morality, reasoning, and negotiations are the drivers to justify much of our decisions.

Part III, Human Influence, presents several characteristics that define human beings, such as human happiness, attention and memory, emotions, credulity, responsibility, reality versus fantasy, egocentricity, judging, and strange reactions.

Human happiness is a sense of well-being, joy, or contentment. When people are enjoying life, feel successful, or safe, or lucky, they feel happiness. Are people happier? Did the wealth humankind accumulated over the last five centuries translate into new-found contentment? Happiness depends on subjective expectations, therefore, it is harder to understand. 'Be true to yourself,' 'Listen to yourself,' 'Follow your heart,' are subjective motivators of happiness. The keys to happiness are in the hands of our biochemical system. Biological happiness is no more and no less than experiencing pleasant bodily sensations. Any meaning that people ascribe to their lives is just a delusion but meaningfulness is a valid criterion for happiness. Buddhist happiness results from processes occurring within one's body, and not from events in the outside world. The key to happiness, according to Buddhism, is to know the truth about yourself – to understand who, or what, you are.

Attention and memory explain human inner difficulties. Humans have clear limitations in paying attention, either noticing someone or identifying something interesting. People are aware only of a small amount of the total information their eyes take in and even less is processed by their conscious mind and remembered. Regarding memory, when we learn a new subject, we start losing the memory of the information after a few days or even months, after a year we may forget everything. People are influenced by the subconscious more than what they believe. Priming happens when a stimulus in the past affects the way people behave and think or the way they perceive another stimulus later on. If a situation is familiar people can fall back on intuition. However, if the situation is novel, people will have to boot up their conscious minds.

Emotions present a summary of human emotions that affect people's behavior. Indignation, resentment, envy, admiration, commitment, and praise are emotions not found in other animals, demonstrate claims for accountability. Resentment, guilt, gratitude, and anger are emotions found in other animals and represent ways in which the demand for accountability is made explicit. Humans demonstrate a dark side that interferes with healthy relationships. We have to distinguish people who are evil from those who are merely bad. Evil people try to destroy others' mindfulness. Evil people are much more dangerous, they are bad and capable of endangering everybody. Emotional non-violent strategies are recommended to avoid severe confrontation. Communities that can resolve their conflicts in this way have a competitive advantage over those whose only response to injury is violence. "The habit of capitulation rather than fighting to the end over territory and mates likewise has a life-preserving and therefore general preserving function." Expressing guilt is another strategy to prevent additional violence. The path of reconciliation is preferable to the eternal pursuit of conflict. Vanity and envy are emotions characteristic of human beings. People depend on emotions to tell if something is good or bad, greatly overestimate rewards and tend to stick on their first impressions. The origin of certain emotional states is unavailable to people, and when pressed to explain them, they will just make something up. People's opinion is the result of years of paying attention to information that confirmed what they believed while ignoring information that challenged their preconceived notions. Expectations can be altered to fool experts, consumers, and the population. People depend on the anchoring effect every day to predict the outcome of events, to estimate how much time something will take, or how much money something will cost. The hindsight effect makes people often look back on the things they have just learned and assume they knew them or believed them all along. Unless people consciously keep tabs on their progress, they assume the way they feel now is the way they have always felt, according to consistency bias.

Regarding credulity, most people are superstitious and it does not mean they believe in supernatural forces. Excluding religions, most superstitions are popular beliefs people repeat over and over. Animistic beliefs were common among ancient foragers, places, animals, plants and natural phenomena had awareness and feelings, and could communicate directly with humans. Religions assert that our laws are not the result of human caprice but are ordained by an absolute and supreme authority, and it defines a system of human norms and values. There is a confrontation between science and religion on matters affecting human nature. Myths have been a way of using the notion of superstition into modern societies. The ability to create an imagined reality out of words enabled large numbers of strangers to cooperate effectively. Myths, it transpired, are stronger than anyone could have imagined. Coincidences are nourished by superstitions. People tend to ignore random chance when the results seem meaningful or when people want a random event to have a meaningful cause. Subjective validation increases with superstitions. People are prone to believe that vague statements and predictions are true, especially if they are positive and address them personally. The argument from ignorance is supported by superstitions. When people are unsure of something, they are more likely to accept strange explanations. Apophenia is supported by superstitions. Coincidences are a routine part of life, even the seemingly miraculous ones. Thinking of having control of random events is influenced by superstitions. People often believe they have control over outcomes that are either random or are too complex to predict.

Responsibility is the feeling of holding each other accountable for what they do and it includes ourselves. Responsibility involves rights, deserts, and duties. For humans, the field of obligation is wider than the field of choice. Like any other behavioral characteristic, responsibility depends on the context and the interpretation of the duties. Procrastination enters the realm of responsibility. It is fueled by weakness in the face of impulse and a failure to think about thinking. Procrastination is an impulse; it's buying fresh bread every time even if you already got lots of bread at home. The bystander effect is fueled by a misinterpretation of responsibility where the group becomes irresponsible. The more people who witness a person in distress, the less likely it is that anyone will help.

How do we separate fantasy from reality? How can we be sure the story of our life both from long ago and minute to minute is true? There is a pleasant vindication to be found when people accept they can't. Human beings are usually deluded regarding reality and fantasy. Confabulation is created by the misunderstanding between reality and fantasy. People are often ignorant of their motivations and create fictional narratives to explain their decisions, emotions, and history without realizing it. The just-world fallacy is fueled by our misunderstanding of reality. It establishes that the beneficiaries of good fortune often do nothing to earn it, and bad people often get away with their actions without consequences. The availability heuristic is supported by reality considerations. People are far more likely to believe something is commonplace if they can find one example of it.

Humans are primarily egocentrics and they have no choice. Self-serving bias is fueled by egocentric instincts. People use to have a positive appreciation of themselves that tends to be overly exaggerated. The actual moment and the past are remembered differently. People are multiple selves, and happiness is based on satisfying all of them. The representativeness heuristic is an egocentric misinterpretation of reality. People jump to conclusions based on how representative a person seems to be of a preconceived character type. The argument from authority is an egocentric misinterpretation of what other people represent. The status and credentials of an individual greatly influence their perception of that individual's message. The spotlight effect is an egocentric view of ourselves and people devote little attention to others unless they are prompted to. Conformity is an egocentric characteristic that makes us yield. It takes little more than an authority figure or social pressure to get people to obey because conformity is a survival instinct. The straw man fallacy is an egocentric position of superiority. In any argument, anger will tempt people to reframe their opponent's position.

Judgment, both conscious and unconscious, is a fundamental part of the human experience. People do it around the clock because it's a necessary function of moving, acting, and living in a dynamic world. Actions and intentions define partially how judgment proceeds. Placing importance on intentions allows you to be patient and kind and expect the same from others while focusing on actions is a great motivator to try hard and hold both people and yourself accountable. The connection between morality and religion is not an accident, as persons, we make ourselves accountable for our actions and states of mind. Human societies are communities of persons, who live in mutual judgment, organizing their world in terms of moral concepts. People might be great judges of character, but they need to be great judges of evidence to avoid delusion. People easily forget about the power of the setting when judging others. The ad hominem fallacy is a way of judging the person instead of the idea. What someone says and why they say it should be judged separately. The third-person effect is a way of judging to defend others. People believe their opinions and decisions are based on experience and facts, while those who disagree with them are falling for the lies and propaganda of sources people don't trust. The Dunning-Kruger effect is a judgment mechanism to defend ourselves. People are generally pretty bad at estimating their competence and the difficulty of complex tasks. The attribution error is a judging mechanism that forgets the context. Other people's behavior is more the result of the situation than their disposition.

Strange reactions are a characteristic of humans. Humans are the most bizarre creatures in the animal kingdom. The proof is in the many gross, unnecessary, contradictory and simply inexplicable things they do. Lying is common and is likely linked to several psychological factors. Foremost among these factors is self-esteem. Like it or not, gossip is a part of everyday life. Scientists speculate that gossip may bring humans closer together. Boredom isn't really about keeping people busy. Boredom stems from an objective lack of neurological excitement, creating dissatisfaction, frustration or disinterest. Contrary to folk wisdom, most laughter is not about humor; it is about relationships between people. When we laugh, we're often communicating playful intent. And the more laughter there is, the more bonding occurs within the groups. Normalcy bias is a human strange reaction that makes people freeze. People become abnormally calm and pretend everything is normal in a crisis. Self-handicapping is another strange reaction making people cautious over possible outcomes. People often create conditions for failure ahead of time to protect their ego. Learned helplessness is a strange reaction making people accept bad situations. If people feel they are not in control of their destiny, they will give up and accept whatever situation they are in. Catharsis is a strange reaction in the sense that people shouldn't vent their anger because venting people's anger increases aggressive behavior over time. Supernormal releasers are strange reactions people show on special occasions produced by overstimulation. If people associate something with survival but find an example of that thing that is more perfect than anything our ancestors could have ever dreamed of – it will overstimulate them.

Part IV, Evaluating Socialism, uses the Behavioral Framework to organize the findings of socialism's performance.

Regarding life motivators related to socialism, staying eternally in power, copying communism, ideological background, non-humanistic approach, religious inspiration, blaming capitalism, absence of science, fabricating heroes, ignorance on evolution, fantasy-based explanations, and missing on diversity.

Doing or acting characteristics are related to the use of language, the management of groups, socialist's new order, the understanding of happiness and misery, the implementation of the state, manipulating the poor, exploiting obedience, accepting sufferings, implementing gossip, planning boredom, using laughter, inaction in crisis, and convincing people.

Personal influences, exploiting emotions, hiring liars, promoting envy, venting anger, suspecting individuality, misunderstanding happiness, hiding reality, cheer up superstitions, arguing from ignorance, benefit from weaknesses, important people archetypes, attacking the person, trust and truth confusion, and pessimistic approach.

Social influences, cooperation, collectivization, human rights, the strategy of lies, evil socialism, vague statements, highly gifted socialists, socialist inexperience, lack of context.

Justification characteristics of socialism, hiding results, third party effect, ignorance facilitates socialism, exploiting obedience, misunderstood equality, despotic socialism, non-capitalist happiness, blaming others, first impressions, lack of risk and benefits, punishing failure, few successes, required honesty, misinterpreting failures, hiding statistics, critics to the opposition, explaining failures, socialist incapacity, active opposition, and rejecting socialism.

Germinal Boloix

Part I: Background

To tackle the relationship between socialism and human nature, a good knowledge of both subjects is required. Socialism and specifically Absurd Socialism has been the subject of many books, including the series written by the author on that matter [Boloix 2017] [Boloix 2018] [Boloix 2019]. Human nature has been discussed in depth by psychologists for many years. However, the relationship between socialism and human nature has been mostly absent in the literature.

This part of the book presents basic concepts related to socialism and human nature. Most of the concepts reflect the view that human nature must be related to political systems, that to design a political system we must first understand human nature. It is absurd to devise a political system proposing the creation of a new human creature without human nature comprehension. Humans are diverse and complicated, there is no unique understanding of the characteristics of a person. Socialism is characterized by pursuing the construction of a new creature, invented in the mind of a bunch of improvisers, following a limited understanding of the concept of the person.

Socialism has a poor understanding of reality, socialists dream of a new world just and full of solidarity. It is clear that it is impossible to change humans, they are going to maintain their virtues and defects independently of political systems. Therefore, a political system must take into consideration all human weaknesses. To improve the world it is necessary to understand its complexity and understand how it works.

A political system must thrive for improvement under the premise that it will never be perfect, there is no perfection in any structure devised by humans. We must be satisfied with imperfect approaches directed to help the life of the population. Socialism is misguided when it insists in serving just part of the population, the political system must help all those important partners that contribute in one way or another to promote prosperity, including workers and the rich.

There is a need for regulations to design a functional world, there is no doubt about that. However, socialism proposes regulations based on false premises. Regulating free enterprising or private property and giving totalitarian power to the state are measures that constrain the contribution of citizens. Regulations to promote work and productivity should be the real motivators in a society.

Socialism has always claimed the importance of groups in solving everyday problems. Socialists must understand the limitations of groups; not everything can be done in groups and groups are not required to function all the time. The combination of individuals and groups is the right approach, individuals can bring ideas into groups and groups can collaborate to define the final approach to follow.

Cult culture has been a common approach pursued by humans, it is common to find family members or religious worshipers getting together to organize their activities. However, cult culture has its limitations, crossing a certain threshold the cult starts to crumble. Socialism wants to apply its doctrine at the level of the country or even at the level of the world. It is impossible to apply the same approach to everybody and socialism collapses under its weight.

Human values should be understood independently of political systems. It is unfair to treat a capitalist as egoist or greedy just because he works hard to grind for the future. A capitalist is just another human being with needs and having an interpretation of how the world must be. Human values should not be submissive to the desires of a political system, human values must go first and the political system must kneel in front of them. Socialism is a system that puts human values in second rank, first is the consolidation of the Utopia and then, maybe, after hundreds of years, the satisfaction of human values.

Finally, the case of Venezuela is documented to demonstrate the failure of the socialist approach. The case of Venezuela is pathetic, a country with human and natural resources in the hands of a bunch of adventurers with a failed political approach. Venezuela followed sectarian policies to limit individual freedom, free enterprising and private property, disgruntling agriculture and manufacturing, and creating an impoverished population considered in a worse situation than the case of Zimbabwe.

Chapter 1: Socialism and Reality

The term socialism was originally applied to a political-economic system with public ownership of large industries and corporations. Socialism is both political theory and a political-economic system that emphasizes the duty of society to ensure social and economic fairness and equality. In pure socialist theory, this means that society, or rather the government, should own and/or control the means of production, private property, and wealth, all of which have to be used for the benefit of everyone and not simply for the benefit of a rich individual or a privileged minority. [Fleming 2008]

Socialists and communists have always dreamed of constructing a new society, a Utopian ideal that can never be attained. There are many reasons why that ideal cannot be attained, however, the main reason is their misunderstanding of human nature. Throughout the second half of the twentieth century, socialism came to be associated more with the welfare state and with step-by-step improvements in the living conditions of the majority of citizens than with an entirely new social order. [Brown 2009]

There are other concepts such as equality for all and fair justice for all that have been misinterpreted by socialism. Everybody wants to do good under the right circumstances. However, people are different, some are good and others are bad, and worst of all, people are good and bad at the same time. Some people demonstrate more than others their will to do good, whereas some other people demonstrate their evil nature depending on the context. Equality and justice are two concepts that require human nature understanding.

Beware of socialists, appeals to ideological principles and rights are generally a cover. People must be suspicious of the socialist's motives. There is always some principled way to defend any position, especially one's interests. Both freedom and stability are principled positions (the good reason) selectively asserted depending upon how we like the leader (the real reason). In devising fixes to the world's ills, the essential first step is to understand what the protagonists want and how different policies and changes will affect their welfare. A reformer who takes what people say at face value will quickly find their reforms at a dead end. [Bueno 2011]

Who does not appreciate a better society? Who does not admire an improved human? Who does not dream of an economic system without pressures? Who does not respect the self-determination of the individual? Everybody does. However, solutions must be viable, charlatans abound and socialism has become the more distrusted approach to choose. Socialists say there is not yet an example of a real socialist society, in the same way, capitalists can say capitalism is still in its developmental stages. Democracy and capitalism are not perfect systems, perfection does not exist. Capitalism has taken hundreds of years to evolve and even with weaknesses has been able to maintain a decent society over the years.

According to socialists, "Socialism means a new form of society and a new form of human consciousness, free from the distorting pressures of capitalism. Only in this way will the human capacity for self-determination finally become a reality." Socialists have found in capitalism a common enemy to fight against. Capitalism is the sinner of all human problems and socialists praise their approach as flawless.

Aiming at capitalism as the evil to conquer, socialists and communists have always look for ways of redistributing income, taking from some to give to others, instead of putting people to work. Any human being must move to find something to eat, most of them work to get something to eat, it is a natural way of surviving. Any society must transmit this desire to work to all the citizens. Welfare should be minimal provided people are healthy and strong. People must justify their need for welfare. Notions of welfare in socialism, include a system of taxation to transfer wealth from the more affluent classes to the less affluent and to establish systems to provide pensions (social security) and health care, either for the poor or for the entire population. [Fleming 2008]

Socialists promote unproven assessments, such as the problems of societies are originated in the capitalist approach instead of on human nature considerations. Capitalists are guilty of all the disgraces of humanity: War? In capitalism, it's human nature to fight. Racism? Capitalism promotes racism and it's human nature to fear "outsiders," or "dissimilar." Women's oppression? Capitalists are misogynistic, they maintain men and women are "naturally different." For socialists, it is possible to blame anything on capitalism. They have not been capable of producing their viewpoint to support human's particular characteristics.

It is clear that Christians were the first promoters of socialist ideas, which by themselves are not bad, but placed in the context of society are rather harmful. Excluding the belief in a 'human god' and the myth of Jesus as the son of that human god, Christian principles may be acceptable. Collective ownership of the means of production and sharing of property have been two pillars of socialism and communism for hundreds of years. Christians were the first to claim that property should be public instead of private. Common possessions were looked upon by many of the first Christians as an ideal to be aimed at. The disciples of Jesus 'were of one heart and one soul: neither said any of them that ought of the things which he possessed was his own, but they had all things common.' [Brown 2009]

Without the help of the priests and the participation of worshipers, Christianity would not exist. There must be a reason why Christianity is still popular and one of the reasons is that it takes into consideration human nature. The relationship between socialism and human nature should answer the question of the popularity of socialism. There are many fantasies socialists use to convince people to join their cause, "Everybody will work happily for the good of everybody," "We are going to be all equal," "The rich will disappear and the poor will reign." Some intellectuals and common people have contributed to maintaining a wrongful socialist approach alive; intellectuals live in a fantasy, and common people have no clue what socialism means.

The trend of Latin American autocratic and authoritarian governments using democracy as a tool in the process of creating socialist dictatorships exposes critical flaws of democracy as a system of government. The replication of these regimes reveals not only the personal ambition or abuse of power of the leaders, but also the eventual dissembling of democratic values (freedom of expression), principles (separation of powers), and institutions (free vote) that once inspired, and are synonymous with the notion of democracy. [Gaona 2018]

Among the many pitfalls of socialism let us review the way it wants to improve the world, the way it interprets how to manage the common good, the interpretation of the need of regulations in a society, the way cooperation is excessively imposed, its orientation towards a cult-oriented society, and its twisted imagined society.

An example of a country destroyed by socialism is Venezuela, submerged in Absurd Socialism. Why are there still some people pushing for such kinds of wrongful socialist ideals that have been for a long time erroneous?

Improving the World

Humans want to improve the world but they must first understand how. What are the world forces into play? What are the motivations of people? What are the objectives of humankind? It is not acceptable to make people miserable in the name of an absurd idea. Humans need to understand human nature and diversity. Humans are imperfect and society must consider that. Societies are imagined by humans, therefore, let us come up with realistic solutions to real problems.

To improve the world, all of us must first suspend faith in conventional wisdom. Let logic and evidence be the guide and our eyes will be opened to the reasons why the world works the way it does. Knowing how and why things are as they are is a first, crucial step toward learning how to make a better world. [Bueno 2011]

The world has many deficiencies, there are too many difficulties: how to make a living, how to be happy, how to succeed, how to attain justice, are just some examples of shortcomings humans endure during their life. We all know how injustices in every realm of human life proliferate. However, some people still believe it is possible to improve the world and live in a 'Just World' such that they can live happily and secure forever.

Even though it is a good idea to struggle for a 'Just World,' at the same time we must understand that it is impossible to attain perfection. People must accept world deficiencies but push for a better human future. It is preferable an imperfect solution that works than an unattainable fantasy. People should never let the quest for perfection block the way to lesser improvement. Utopian dreams of a perfect world are just that: Utopia. Pursuing the perfect world for everyone is a waste of time and an excuse for not doing the hard work of making the world better for many. [Bueno 2011]

Making the world better is a difficult task. If it were not, then it would already have been done. The misery in which so many people live would already have been overcome. The enrichment of CEOs while their stockholders lose their shirts would be a thing of the past. However, the inherent problem with change is that improving the life for one group generally means making at least some other persons worse off. New leaders of the latter group will raise if change really will solve the people's problems. [Bueno 2011]

The Tragedy of the Commons
The tragedy of the commons is an idea suggesting people aren't very good at sharing. Imagine a mountain full of rabbits. Only a few people know about it. They agree to take just as many rabbits from the mountain as each needs to eat. As long as everyone takes just what they need, the mountain will stay full of rabbits.

One day, someone happens to notice one of the others has started taking more than he or she needs and is selling the extra rabbits in a nearby town. Eventually, that person has a better trap or rifle than the others. What do people do? If they start over hunting too, each one will also be able to get a better rifle, maybe even a small all-terrain vehicle. Maybe some of them could partner up against the cheater. Maybe everyone will just start taking as many rabbits as desired. Maybe someone could just tell the world about the mountain. All of these scenarios will probably lead to the ruin of the common good. If people do nothing, the mountain will still be able to support most of them, but the cheater wins. Anger over unfair situations is something people can't help but feel.

In situations like the imaginary mounting above, in an effort not to fall behind, everyone loses. A big holiday meal, for example, can become a zero-sum game if everyone piles a plate, but if everyone takes only what he or she needs, everyone wins. The tragedy of taking from a common good is over time how the common good will be depleted out of just a tiny amount of greed. One misguided exploiter can crash the system. And greed is contagious.

Cheating and Slacking
Many believe that the world would be better if there were fewer cheaters and slackers. Work is an affirmative activity that keeps people busy in a productive and useful context. However, human beings are always looking for alternative paths to make their life easy, even if it implies worsening the life of others. Cheaters can ruin the system, not by themselves, but because the infectious nature of their gluttony is spread as people catch on to being shortchanged.

When people see others cheating they automatically think about the possibility of cheating without considering the consequences. Some people see systems like welfare or affirmative action as disrupting the balance of the natural world. Slackers, they think, would get what they deserve if the government kept their noses out of it. Their bad karma would come around to crush them, but unnatural forces prevent it.

The old emotional brain kicks in, however, when people see cheating. It's an innate response that served our ancestors well. People know deep down that cheaters must be punished because it takes only one cheater to make the economy sputter out. People would rather lose the game than helping someone who isn't helping them.

Purely logical creatures could be trusted but people are not purely logical creatures. People will cheat if they think the system is cheating them. The urge to help others and discourage cheating is something that helped primates as us survive in small groups for millions of years, but when the system becomes gigantic and abstract, like the budget for a nation or the welfare system for an entire state, it becomes difficult to make sense of the world through those old evolutionary behaviors.

Need for Regulations (The Public Goods Game)

Without some form of regulation, slackers and cheaters will crash economic systems because people don't want to feel like suckers. It isn't true that we could create a system with no regulations where everyone would contribute to the good of society, everyone would benefit, and everyone would be happy. So what about public goods, things which everyone contributes to instead of taking from? It looks like the tragedy of the commons is true. Research into human behavior shows people are not so smart when it comes to contributing to the public good. [McRaney 2011]

The public good game can be associated, among many other alternatives, with paying taxes. If everybody pays taxes, the society gets the benefits of better services. However, there are always some people who don't want to contribute and the services start getting worse. The crazy thing about this game is how illogical it is to stop contributing just because someone in the group is free riding. If everyone else is still being a good citizen, everyone will still win. This game is sometimes used to illustrate how regulation is necessary to keep any sort of nonprofit public good alive. Streetlights would never get put along dark roads, and bridges would collapse if people weren't forced to pay taxes.

The public goods game suggests regulation through punishment discourages slackers. It isn't true people don't want to help; they just don't want to help a cheater or do more work than a slacker – even if not helping leads to ruin the game for them and everyone else. The tragedy of the commons can be used to encourage people to take care of their piece of the world, but they might think not everyone is going to buy a fuel-efficient car and recycle plastic, so why should they?

Some people play by the rules, pay taxes, and sacrifice hours of life for overtime pay, they assume their karma has to be for a reason. Their pursuit of the good life can't be futile. The rich, they think, must deserve what they have, they work hard and produce benefits. One day, people who play by the rules will be lifted even higher up in the social hierarchy to join the others who have what they deserve for their hard work.

Cooperation

Humans are completely different from primates when cooperation is demanded. Human beings have a unique ability to cooperate in large, well-organized groups and employ a complex morality that relies on reputation and punishment. Although our willingness to cooperate depends on the circumstances (after all, we may also kill those who do not belong to our group), primates in nature are mostly competitive between groups. [de Wall 2014]

It is very difficult for a human being to live in isolation. It is hard to do everything to survive individually. It is easy to live close to a community and human beings survive in particularly favorable conditions, created by cooperative living. These conditions involve cooperation and the division of labor. Individuals use to subordinate themselves to the group, ensuring the existence of the species. Division of labor (which is another way of saying civilization) is the only capable of ensuring that the tools of survival are available to humankind. Cooperation is the best guarantor of the continued existence of human beings! [Adler 1992]

'Cooperation' sounds very altruistic, but it is not always voluntary and seldom egalitarian. Most human cooperation networks have been geared toward oppression and exploitation. The peasants paid for the burgeoning cooperation networks with their precious food surpluses, despairing when the tax collector wiped out an entire year of hard labor with a single stroke of his imperial pen. The famed Roman amphitheaters were often built by slaves so that wealthy and idle Romans could watch other slaves engage in vicious gladiatorial combat. Even prisons and concentration camps are cooperation networks and can function only because thousands of strangers somehow manage to coordinate their actions. [Harari 2014]

Cult Culture (Cult Indoctrination)

Cult indoctrination is a characteristic of socialism. Cults are populated by people just like anybody. It isn't true that people are too smart to join a cult. [McRaney 2011]

Cults are a side effect of natural human tendencies. People have an innate desire to belong to a group and to hang out with other interesting people. If you have ever admired someone you have never actually met – like a musician or philosopher – you've experienced the seed of the cult phenomenon. If you cheer for your local basketball team, The Raptors, for example, you are experiencing the cult factor.

The research on cults suggests you don't usually join for any particular reason; you just sort of fall into them the way you fall into any social group. After all, when did you join your circle of friends? Your group of close friends has likely changed a great deal over the years, but have you made many active choices concerning who you hang out with other than avoiding the ones who are a pain in the ass?

The sorts of people who join cults are not all insecure or emotionally weak. People would like to think they are not the sort of person who could be beguiled by a charismatic leader with a clear vision. Cults form around sparkly, interesting individuals – Marx, Lenin, Fidel Castro, Kim Il Sung, Hugo Chavez – but people don't usually follow the leader, they follow the ideals the leader proclaims to be serving.

As primates, people are keenly aware of group dynamics. People are hardwired to want to hang out with other people and associate with groups. Survival has depended on it for millions of years. Besides, people don't evaluate their behavior and choices and feelings to understand who they are. Instead, people have an idealistic vision of themselves, a character they have dreamed up in their minds, and people are always trying to become this character. People seek out groups to affiliate with to better solidify who they are in the story they tell themselves – the story explaining why people do the things they do.

Cults start with a charismatic individual. Maybe this person believes he is special in some way, or maybe he is just naturally interesting. Well, he might even be a charlatan and some people still follow him. People start hanging out with him, and a spontaneous group forms with the charismatic person becoming an authority figure. If this person has an agenda or a goal, or enemies he wants to be eliminated, he will cultivate the goodwill of his fans into action. If he has difficult goals to reach, he will try to expand his group with recruitment or proselytizing, often hiding his true intentions so as not to scare away potential members. Some leaders know what they are doing, but some just serve their instincts and accidentally form cults around themselves before they realize what they've done. How these people wield their power over others ultimately determines how history will label them.

The Venezuelan Case

Venezuela is a small country in South America that followed one of the worsts interpretations of socialism (Absurd Socialism) taken from experiences from the Soviets, China's Mao, North Korea, Nazi Germany, Zimbabwe, and Cuba.

"Oil is the Devil's excrement," according to Juan Pablo Perez Alfonzo, a Venezuelan who founded the Organization of Petroleum Exporting Countries (OPEC), the cartel of oil-producing nations. "Ten years from now, twenty years from now, you will see: oil will bring us to ruin." And he was right. Extracting revenue from the land itself provides a convenient alternative, cutting the people out of the equation altogether. [Bueno 2011]

Absurd Socialism is a non-viable approach and the chronology of events that led to Venezuela's destruction is summarized as follows:

- People were tired of current politicians. Many years of democracy did not convince people that the problems were being solved
- Hugo Chavez participated in an unsuccessful coup d'etat that made him famous on TV after many years plotting in the military
- Hugo Chavez participated in general elections promising to fight corruption and poverty and because people opted for a new face, different from the same old politicians, he became president
- A new constitution was approved one year later. The constitution was written with several loopholes to allow multiple interpretations and was unclear on many important articles such as how to get rid of a bad government. Everything had to be solved through fraudulent referendums and elections that took years to implement
- The Congress, composed of two chambers, senators and MPs, was abolished and changed to one assembly with several MPs
- Hugo Chavez started to get control of all the institutions in the country. He started by taking charge of the electoral power and placing his partisans on top of the hierarchy

- Military personnel started to take charge of many institutions at all levels of government with the approval of Hugo Chavez. The military was basically in charge of running the country. Corruption spread out fast all over the institutions of the country thanks to this totalitarian power
- Hugo Chavez continued to name his partisans and military personnel in charge of food and medicine distribution. The leader started to force the judiciary system to make decisions according to his wishes; over time his wishes were obeyed. He named himself the leader of the revolution
- The constitution was kidnapped and interpreted to serve the regime; it was violated on several occasions to fit the leader's viewpoint. The rule by law was implemented, laws were written to fit the desires of the leader
- The leader of the revolution started expropriating business, land, buildings, and banks in the name of his revolution
- Hugo Chavez decided to lay off about 20 thousand employees from the oil industry at the time of the oil strike. He put the oil industry under his mandate and made the industry deteriorate
- Precise instructions were given to public administration officers to penalize any opposition to his government. It included layoffs and lower salaries to dissidents
- In the meantime, the price of oil, the main source of income, skyrocketed over the one hundred dollar mark for many years
- Hugo Chavez took control of the central bank and abolished free currency exchange. All financial transactions had to be approved by the government
- Hugo Chavez was in charge of administering a personal budget of the same amount of the country's yearly budget. Nobody knew how it was spent
- Businesses had to ask for permission from the government to bring in imports. Many industries had to close because there were no raw materials for manufacturing
- After the death of the leader of the revolution, the new president elected from the same party in power started to mismanage the resources of the country
- Lack of food, medicines, and services started to spread out. A hyperinflation process started to build up making Venezuela the worse economic performer in the world

- The honorable National Assembly was elected with a majority of the opposition
- The constitution continued to be violated again on several occasions to serve the regime dictatorial nature. A fraudulent National Constitutional Assembly was named to work on a new constitution
- People's protests were fought with weapons and bullets and hundreds of dissidents were killed
- Hundreds of political opponents were jailed
- Nicolas Maduro was reelected through fraudulent elections approved by the National Constitutional Assembly
- The government, including the military, has been associated with corruption and drug trafficking for many years
- Many government officials, including the president and his family, have been banned from international financial institutions and their accounts frozen
- Because the election of Nicolas Maduro was fraudulent, an impasse has been created and a parallel government with the leadership of the honorable National Assembly has been in charge of ending usurpation, establish a transitional government, and call new elections
- More than ten months down the road, the parallel government has not been able to end usurpation and the social situation is getting worse

Absurd Socialism has been applied in a few countries, including Venezuela, and the results are clear, destruction and hunger. It is a common pattern that first uses democracy, then makes people believe in improvement, and at the end justify a tyrant in the name of change. Cuba is the main failure in Latin America. There are other countries, such as Nicaragua, Bolivia, Argentina, Ecuador, and Mexico, which may follow similar paths to destruction, using the excuse of socialism and imposing authoritarian regimes.

Chapter 2: Human Evolution

Psychology and anthropology have given many contributions to understand human nature. Psychology is the science that studies people's behavior whereas anthropology is the science that studies social interactions. According to evolutionary psychologists, basic features of human psychology were hardwired into the brains of our ancestors by natural selection to enable them to survive the conditions during the early evolution. Anthropology explores how people lived and try to understand how the world around them affected their survival. For tens of thousands of years our ancestors required individual survival capabilities and social interactions to thrive; human nature evolved through adaptation to current conditions.

The evolution of the universe has made humans a certain way, according to natural laws, instead of another, imagined, theological way. Humans have followed irremediable biological evolution and adapted to the harsh environment. Depending on their inborn nervous and neural structure, humans are capable of survival and improvement in their life; their intellect allows them to solve everyday problems faster and better.

Human evolution is not known in its full dimension and human nature is definitively related to the development of the universe. Harsh conditions, mutations, and natural selection have affected the behavior of individuals to benefit themselves and their immediate relatives, therefore, human nature bends us to the imperatives of selfishness and tribalism. [Wilson 1978]

Humans evolved biologically during millions of years whereas cultural evolution has just started to be understood. Biological evolution is known through archaeology, using the study of human remains as the source of information. Therefore, biological evolution can explain just a tiny part of human evolution. Cultural evolution has been unknown for hundreds of thousands of years, there is no tangible proof of how was our behavior during those years. Humans have gone through difficult periods over their evolution while trying to survive. Historically, human interactions are not known in its entirety, only the last ten thousand years have been recorded in some way or another. Societies, such as the ones we know today, only started to exist during the last two thousand years of human history. Therefore, human understanding of these circumstances is still in progress.

Biology sets the basic parameters for the behavior and capacities of Homo sapiens. The ability to make and use tools has been with us for millions of years. Physiologically, there has been no significant improvement in our tool-making capacity over the last 30,000 years. Genetically, humans and their associated species are almost identical. Genes created the brain that generates the mind from which our thoughts spring. Thus, genetically, human's physical life is as similar to everyone else's as nails in their fingertips. However, their mental life can differ considerably from one to another.

Externally, there are a few biological differences between humans. People look externally the same, they do similar activities, they behave approximately the same but they are behaviorally different. People are not the same, and the failure to notice this can be misinterpreted and twisted to serve certain dangerous ideals. Add to the mix cultural constraints and people definitively differ. Culturally, people are used to certain sets of constraints and experiences in their particular environments shape them all. The similarities between the early civilizations of Egypt, Mesopotamia, India, China, Mexico, and Central and South America are remarkably close; it means they followed similar patterns independently. The parallelism in the major features of the organization is the theory of the dual-track of human social evolution. Nationalism and racism are the culturally nurtured outgrowths of simple tribalism. [Wilson 1978]

Band changed to tribes, true male leaders appeared and gained dominance, alliances between neighboring groups were strengthened and formalized. With still denser populations came the attributes of generic chiefdom: the formal distinction of rank according to membership in families, the hereditary consolidation of leadership, a sharper division of labor, and the redistribution of wealth under the control of the ruling elite. The changes that transpired in the interval from the hunter-gatherer life of forty thousand years ago to the first glimmering of civilization in the Sumerian city-states were created by cultural rather than genetic evolution. The emergence of civilization followed a definable sequence.

The transition to agriculture began around 9500 – 8500 BC in southeastern Turkey, western Iran, and the Levant. It began slowly and in a restricted geographical area. Independently, people in Central America domesticated maize and beans without knowing anything about wheat and pea cultivation in the Middle East. South Americans learned how to raise potatoes and llamas, unaware of what was going on in either Mexico or the Levant. [Harari 2014]

With the move to permanent villages and the increase in the food supply, the population began to grow. Giving up the nomadic lifestyle enabled women to have a child every year. Babies were weaned at an earlier age – they could be fed on porridge and gruel. The extra hands were sorely needed in the fields. But the extra mouths quickly wiped out the food surpluses, so even more fields had to be planted. In most agricultural societies at least one out of every three children died before reaching twenty. Yet the increase in births still outpaced the increase in deaths; humans kept having larger numbers of children. [Harari 2014]

People worked harder, but people did not foresee that the number of children would increase, meaning that the extra wheat would have to be shared between more children. Neither did the early farmers understand that feeding children with more porridge and less breast milk would weaken their immune system and that permanent settlements would be hotbeds for infectious diseases. Nor did the farmers foresee that in good years their bulging granaries would tempt thieves and enemies, compelling them to start building walls and doing guard duty. [Harari 2014]

The division of labor was an important cultural advantage that helped our ancestors become more productive. The division of labor was the skill that allowed Sapiens to improve in so many areas of their communal life; the creation of language and the activity of cooking are just two examples. The language was improved over thousands of years thanks to the work of some people that had the time to do it. Cooking was a skill that some humans improved by dedicating effort to nourish their families.

The Cognitive Revolution is the point when history declared its independence from biology. Homo sapiens started doing very special things. Until the Cognitive Revolution, the doings of all human species belonged to the realm of biology. The period from about 70,000 years ago to about 30,000 years ago constitutes the Cognitive Revolution, it witnessed the invention of boats, oil lamps, bows and arrows and needles (essential for sewing warm clothing). [Harari 2014]

The Mind and The Brain

Descriptions of the brain and its different components have the purpose of clarifying how humans behave. Our brains are not merely devices for mediating between stimulus and response but instruments that enable us to think about and perceive the world and which lead us at times to think about it and perceive it wrongly. [Scruton 2017]

A brain is a biological machine of one hundred billion neurons and the mind can somehow be explained as the summed activity of a finite number of chemical and electrical reactions limiting the human prospect – we are biological and our souls cannot fly free. Is it possible that humans have been hard-wired by evolution to be an all-purpose device, adaptable through learning to any mode of social existence? Human behavior explained from 250 genes to one hundred billion neurons to an unknown potential variety of social systems? [Wilson 1978]

People feel like a single person with a single brain, but in many ways, they are at least two. Thoughts, memories, and emotions cascade throughout the whole, but some tasks are handled better by one side of the brain than the other. Language, for example, is usually a task handled by the left side of the brain, but then bounced back and forth between the two.

How does the mind work, and beyond that why does it work in such a way and not another, and from these two considerations together, what is humans' ultimate nature? Somewhere in the mind, "there is a hard, irreducible, stubborn core of biological urgency, and biological necessity, and biological reason, that culture cannot reach and that reserves the right, which sooner or later it will exercise, to judge the culture and resist and revise it." [Wilson 1978]

The mind can be divided into automatic, emotional, and rational spheres of thought. Let's reduce them to two, the conscious and the unconscious minds (related to the emotional and rational brain). Decisions about risk and reward begin in the unconscious; it notices things as either bad or good, dangerous or safe before the conscious mind can put those feelings into words. Keep in mind how powerful an influence people's mood is on the decision making regions of their mind.

The unconscious mind, related to the emotional brain, is old and powerful but its function can't be directly observed or communicated to consciousness. Instead, the output is mostly intuition and feeling. It is always there in the background co-processing our mental life. "People know more than they know." It is a mistake to believe that the rational mind is in control, the rational mind is oblivious to the influence of the unconscious.

The three main subjects that define the logical components of the mind are cognitive bias, heuristics, and logical fallacies. Life is not always lived under the best conditions. Cognitive biases are predictable patterns of thought and behavior that may lead people to draw incorrect conclusions. Cognitive biases may lead to poor choices, bad judgments, and wacky insights that are often totally incorrect. For example, people tend to look for information that confirms their beliefs and ignore information that challenges them.

Heuristics are mental shortcuts that are used to solve common problems. They speed up processing in the brain but sometimes make people think so fast that they miss what is important. Some heuristics are learned, and others come free with every copy of the human brain. When they work, they help people's mind to stay frugal. When they don't, people see the world as a much simpler place than it is.

Logical fallacies are like math problems involving language, in which people skip a step or get turned around without realizing it. They are arguments in people's minds where a conclusion is reached without realizing it. Logical fallacies can also be the result of wishful thinking. Sometimes people apply good logic to false premises; at other times people apply bad logic to the truth.

Language

Human's most important information to be conveyed was about other humans and not only about the rest of the world. Homo sapiens are social animals, cooperation is their key for survival and reproduction. Their language evolved as a way of gossiping and personal exchange. It was not enough for individual men and women to know the whereabouts of lions and bison. It was much more important for them to know who in their band hated whom, who was sleeping with whom, who was honest, and who was a cheat. [Harari 2014]

To get information out of one head and into another, it has to be transmitted through some sort of communication channel. Faces, sounds, gestures, and words are tools used to allow messages to flow in the transmission process. The huge discrepancy between what people think others understand and what they do has probably led to all sorts of mistakes in everyday communications. Often, people have to back up and restate what they said, or answer questions about the tone, or reword everything and send the message again. Getting an idea out of one head and into another is difficult, and much can be lost in the information transfer. [McRaney 2011]

Yet the truly unique feature of our language is not its ability to transmit information about men and lions. Rather, it's the ability to transmit information about things that do not exist at all. As far as we know, only Sapiens can talk about entire kinds of entities that they have never seen, touched or smelled. There are no gods in the universe, no nations, no money, no human rights, no laws, and no justice outside the common imagination of human beings. The difficulty lies in convincing everyone else to believe a story. How to convince millions of people to believe particular stories about gods, nations, or corporations? The language was the medium to create 'fictions,' 'social constructs,' or 'imagined realities.' [Harari 2014]

<u>Importance of Words</u> (Embodied Cognition)

Embodied cognition stands out the importance of words or symbols. People translate their physical world into words and then believe those words. It isn't true that people's opinions of other people and events are based on objective evaluation. [McRaney 2011]

As strange as this is going to sound, people think in metaphors – words like "warm" and "cold" - "fast" and "slow" - "bright" and "dark." These words have several meanings, "Cold" can be a physical sensation but also a mood, demeanor, or style. "Dark" can describe a shade of color, or the way a sound sounds. Warm sensations bring up word associations that include warmth, and those thoughts prime people to behave in a way that could be metaphorically described as warm.

<u>Schema</u>

People use abstraction to understand complex ideas, places or things. These ideas, or imaginary places, are called a schema. We have a schema for just about everything – pirates, football, microscopes – images and related ideas that orbit the archetypes for objects, scenarios, rooms, and so on. In a typical kitchen, toolbox, bathroom, and other common areas in most homes what do we find? What items would you expect to find in a modern kitchen? Those archetypes form over time as we see examples in life or stories from other people. We also have a schema for places we've never been to, like the bottom of the ocean or ancient Rome.

<u>Knowledge</u>

Sapiens did not forage only for food and materials. They foraged for knowledge as well. To survive, they needed a detailed mental map of their territory. To maximize the efficiency of their daily search for food, they required information about the growth patterns of each plant and the habits of each animal. They needed to know which foods were nourishing, which made you sick, and how to use others as cures. They needed to know the progress of the seasons and what warning signs preceded a thunderstorm or a dry spell. [Harari 2014]

At the individual level, ancient foragers were the most knowledgeable and skillful people in history. The average forager had a wider, deeper and more varied knowledge of her immediate surroundings than most of their modern descendants. Foragers mastered not only the surrounding world of animals, plants, and objects but also the internal world of their bodies and senses.

Our ancestors put a great deal of time and effort into trying to discover the rules that govern the natural world. Humans have sought to understand the universe at least since the Cognitive Revolution. But modern science differs from all previous traditions of knowledge in three critical ways: [Harari 2014]

- The willingness to admit ignorance. Modern science is based on the Latin injunction ignoramus – 'we do not know'. It assumes that we don't know everything. Even more critically, it accepts that the things that we think we know could be proven wrong as we gain more knowledge. No concept, idea or theory is sacred and beyond challenge.

- The centrality of observation and mathematics. Having admitted ignorance, modern science aims to obtain new knowledge. It does so by gathering observations and then using logical and mathematical tools to connect these observations into comprehensive theories.

- The acquisition of new powers. Modern science is not content with creating theories. It uses these theories to acquire new powers, and in particular to develop new technologies.

When particularly complex societies began to appear in the wake of the Agricultural Revolution, a completely new type of information became vital – numbers. Foragers were never obliged to handle large amounts of mathematical data. No forager needed to remember, say, the number of fruit on each tree in the forest. So human brains did not adapt to storing and processing numbers. Yet to maintain a large kingdom, mathematical data was vital. It was never enough to legislate laws and tell stories about guardian gods. One also had to collect taxes. To tax hundreds of thousands of people, it was imperative to collect data about people's incomes and possessions; data about payments made; data about arrears, debts, and fines; data about discounts and exemptions. This added up to millions of data bits, which had to be stored and processed. Without this capacity, the state would never know what resources it had and what further resources it could tap. When confronted with the need to memorize, recall and handle all these numbers, most human brains overdosed or fell asleep. For thousands of years after the Agricultural Revolution, human social networks remained relatively small and simple. The Sumerians invented a system for storing and processing information outside their brains, one that was custom-built to handle large amounts of mathematical data. The data-processing system invented by the Sumerians is called 'writing.' [Harari 2014]

Chapter 3: Social Groupings

Social groups consist of several people who interact, exchange, and identify with one another. A society is composed of several groups interacting with other groups or individuals. The only characteristic of a society that we can be certain of is its incessant change. People have become used to changes, and most of us think about the social order as something flexible, which can be engineered and improved at will. Any attempt to define the characteristics of modern society is akin to defining the color of a chameleon, the society changes over time influenced by knowledge and beliefs.

According to sociologists, a society is a group of people with common territory, some interaction, cultural diversity, and a division of labor to distribute responsibilities. It is impossible to put everybody to interact in society, only some groups interact with other groups making an expansive wave of interactions.

Territory: Most countries have formal boundaries and territory that the world recognizes as theirs. However, a society's boundaries don't have to be geopolitical borders, such as the one between the United States and Canada. Instead, members of society, as well as nonmembers, must recognize particular land as belonging to that society.

Interaction: Members of society must come in contact with one another. If a group of people within a country has no regular contact with another group, those groups become isolated from the rest. Geographic distance and language barriers can separate societies within a country.

Culture: People in a society share aspects of their culture such as language or beliefs. Culture refers to the language, values, beliefs, behavior, and material objects that constitute a people's way of life. It is a defining element of society.

Diversity: Diversity is an important characteristic of any society and it requires an organization to thrive. Human societies are not just groups of cooperating people: they are communities of persons, who live in mutual judgment, organizing their world in terms of moral concepts that arguably have no place in the thoughts of some other primates.

Division of Labor: Division of labor is a vital factor in the maintenance of human society. It gives people the time to participate in different activities instead of living only for survival.

Natural and Imagined Order

We cannot explain the choices that history makes, but we can say something very important about them: history's choices are not made for the benefit of humans. There is absolutely no proof that human well-being inevitably improves as history rolls along. There is no proof that cultures that are beneficial to humans must inexorably succeed and spread, while less beneficial cultures disappear. There is no proof that Christianity was a better choice than Manichaeism, or that the Arab Empire was more beneficial than that of the Sassanid Persians. [Harari 2014]

There is no proof that history is working for the benefit of humans because we lack an objective scale on which to measure such benefit. Different cultures define the good differently, and we have no objective yardstick by which to judge between them. The victors, of course, always believe that their definition is correct. But why should we believe the victors? Christians believe that the victory of Christianity over Manichaeism was beneficial to humankind, but if we do not accept the Christian world view then there is no reason to agree with them. Muslims believe that the fall of the Sassanid Empire into Muslim hands was beneficial to humankind. But these benefits are evident only if we accept the Muslim world view. It may well be that we'd all be better off if Christianity and Islam had been forgotten or defeated. [Harari2014]

In the last two centuries, the currency of politics is that it promises to destroy the old world and build a better one in its place. The main promise of premodern rulers was to safeguard the traditional order or even to go back to some lost golden age. Not even the most conservative of political parties vow merely to keep things as they are. Everybody promises social reform, educational reform, economic reform and they often fulfill those promises. [Harari 2014]

The first millennium BC witnessed the appearance of three potentially universal orders, whose devotees could for the first time imagine the entire world and the entire human race as a single unit governed by a single set of laws. Everyone was 'us,' at least potentially. There was no longer 'them.' The first universal order to appear was economic: the monetary order. The second universal order was political: the imperial order. The third universal order was religious: the order of universal religions such as Buddhism, Christianity, and Islam. [Harari 2014]

A natural order is a stable order. There is no chance that gravity will cease to function tomorrow, even if people stop believing in it. In contrast, an imagined order is always in danger of collapse, because it depends upon myths, and myths vanish once people stop believing in them. To safeguard an imagined order, continuous and strenuous efforts are imperative. Some of these efforts take the shape of violence and coercion. Armies, police forces, courts, and prisons are ceaselessly at work forcing people to act following the imagined order. If an ancient Babylonian blinded his neighbor, some violence was usually necessary to enforce the law of 'an eye for an eye.' When, in 1860, a majority of American citizens concluded that African slaves were human beings and must, therefore, enjoy the right of liberty, it took a bloody civil war to make the southern states acquiesce. [Harari 2014]

However, an imagined order cannot be sustained by violence alone. It requires some true believers as well. Prince Talleyrand, who began his chameleon-like career under Louis XVI, later served the revolutionary and Napoleonic regimes, and switched loyalties in time to end his days working for the restored monarchy, summed up decades of governmental experience by saying that 'You can do many things with bayonets, but it is rather uncomfortable to sit on them.' A single priest often does the work of a hundred soldiers far more cheaply and effectively. Moreover, no matter how efficient bayonets are, somebody must wield them. Why should the soldiers, jailors, judges, and police maintain an imagined order in which they do not believe? Of all human collective activities, the one most difficult to organize is violence. To say that social order is maintained by military force immediately raises the question: what maintains the military order? It is impossible to organize an army solely by coercion. At least some of the commanders and soldiers must truly believe in something, be it God, honor, motherland, manhood or money. [Harari 2014]

This is why cynics don't build empires and why an imagined order can be maintained only if large segments of the population – and in particular large segments of the elite and the security forces – truly believe in it. Christianity would not have lasted 2,000 years if the majority of bishops and priests failed to believe in Christ. American democracy would not have lasted 250 years if the majority of presidents and congressmen failed to believe in human rights. The modern economic system would not have lasted a single day if the majority of investors and bankers failed to believe in capitalism. [Harari 2014]

How do you cause people to believe in an imagined order such as Christianity, socialism, democracy or capitalism? First, you never admit that the order is imagined. You always insist that the order sustaining a society is an objective reality created by the great gods or by the laws of nature. People are unequal, not because Hammurabi said so, but because Enlil and Marduk decreed it. People are equal, not because Thomas Jefferson said so, but because God created them that way. Free markets are the best economic system, not because Adam Smith said so, but because these are the immutable laws of nature. [Harari 2014]

Unfortunately, complex human societies seem to require imagined hierarchies and unjust discrimination. Of course, not all hierarchies are morally identical, and some societies suffered from more extreme types of discrimination than others, yet scholars know of no large society that has been able to dispense with discrimination altogether. Time and again people have created order in their societies by classifying the population into imagined categories, such as superiors, commoners, and slaves; whites and blacks; patricians and plebeians; Brahmins and Shudras; or rich and poor. These categories have regulated relations between millions of humans by making some people legally, politically or socially superior to others. [Harari 2014]

<u>Imagined Communities</u>

All cooperation networks – from the cities of ancient Mesopotamia to the Qin and Roman empires – were 'imagined orders'. The social norms that sustained them were not based on ingrained instincts or personal acquaintances, but rather on belief in shared myths. [Harari 2014]

An imagined community is a community of people who don't know each other but imagine that they do. Such communities are not a novel invention. Kingdoms, empires, and churches functioned for millennia as imagined communities. Like the nuclear family, the community could not completely disappear from our world without any emotional replacement. Markets and states do so by fostering 'imagined communities' that contain millions of strangers, and which are tailored to national and commercial needs. Markets and states today provide most of the material needs once provided by communities, including tribal bonds.

The two most important examples for the rise of such imagined communities are the nation and the consumer band. The nation is the imagined community of the state. The consumer band is the imagined community of the market. Both are imagined communities because it is impossible for all customers in a market or for all members of a nation really to know one another the way villagers knew one another in the past. [Harari 2014]

Consumerism and nationalism work extra hours to make people imagine that millions of strangers belong to the same community, that they all have a common past, common interests, and a common future. This isn't a lie. It's imagination. Like money, limited liability companies and human rights, nations and consumer bands are inter-subjective realities. Imagined communities exist only in people's collective imagination, yet their power is immense. [Harari 2014]

The nation does its best to hide its imagined character. Most nations argue that they are a natural and eternal entity, created in some primordial epoch by mixing the soil of the motherland with the blood of the people. Yet such claims are usually exaggerated. Nations existed in the distant past, but their importance was much smaller than today because the importance of the state was much smaller. A resident of medieval Nuremberg might have felt some loyalty towards the German nation, but she felt far more loyalty towards her family and the local community, which took care of most of her needs. Moreover, whatever importance ancient nations may have had, few of them survived. Most existing nations evolved only after the Industrial Revolution. [Harari 2014]

Group Characteristics

<u>Group Conformity</u> (Groupthink)

Groupthink is a behavior present in groups. The desire to reach consensus and avoid confrontation hinders progress. It isn't true that problems are easier to solve when a group of people gets together to discuss solutions. When a group of people comes together to make a decision, every demon in the psychological bestiary will be summoned. [McRaney 2011]

Conformity, rationalization, stereotyping, delusions of grandeur – they all come out to play, and no one is willing to fight them back into hell because it might lead to abandoning the plan or a nasty argument. Groupthink discourages creativity or individual responsibility during the practice of thinking and making decisions as a group.

No matter what sort of job people have, from time to time everyone has to get together and come up with a plan. Sometimes people do this in small groups, sometimes as an entire company. True groupthink depends on three conditions – a group of people who like one another, isolation, and a deadline for a crucial decision.

Groups survive by maintaining harmony. When everyone is happy and all egos are free from harm it tends to increase productivity. This is true whether people are hunting buffalo or selling televisions. Team spirit, morale, group cohesion – these are golden principles long-held high by managers, commanders, chieftains, and kings. People know instinctively that dissent leads to chaos, so they avoid it.

People are quick to form groups and then feel as if they should defend those groups from the ill wishes of other groups. When groups get together to make a decision, an illusion of invulnerability can emerge in which everyone feels secure in the cohesion. People begin to rationalize other people's ideas and don't reconsider their own. People want to defend the group's cohesion from all harm, so they suppress doubts, they don't argue, they don't offer alternatives – and since everyone is doing this, the leader of the group falsely assumes everyone agrees.

If the group includes a person who can hire or fire, groupthink comes into play. With a boss hanging around, people get nervous. People start observing the other members of the group in an attempt to figure out what the consensus opinion is. Meanwhile, people are simultaneously weighing the consequences of disagreeing. The problem is, every other person in the group is doing the same thing, and if everyone decides it would be a bad idea to risk losing friends or a job, a false consensus will be reached and no one will do anything about it.

It turns out, for any plan to work, every team needs at least one asshole who doesn't give a shit if it gets fired or exiled or excommunicated. For a group to make good decisions, they must allow dissent and convince everyone they are free to speak their minds without the risk of punishment.

<u>Groups are inefficient</u> (Social Loafing)

Social loafing appears in groups of people. Once part of a group, people tend to put in less effort because they know their work will be pooled together with others. It isn't true that when people are joined by others in a task, they work harder and become more accomplished. [McRaney 2011]

When people want to accomplish something big, something that will require a lot of time and efforts like startup business or a short film, their instincts might tell them the more people can be afforded to hire the better the work will be and the faster they will reach their goals. The truth though is when people join the efforts of others toward a common goal, everyone tends to loaf more than if each was working alone. If people know they aren't being judged as individuals, their instinct is to fade into the background.

The more people added, the less effort any one person contributes. People do this all the time, but they don't do it on purpose – well, except when they just mouth the words to the song everyone else is singing. As long as people think they are part of a group, they unconsciously put in less effort. No one realizes it, and no one admits to it. Additionally, there is the consideration of communication overhead, adding more people in a project increases the amount of time required to communicate with others.

Putting less effort is more likely to show up when the task at hand is simple. With complex tasks, it is usually easy to tell who isn't pulling their weight. Once people know their laziness can be seen, they try harder. People do this because of another behavior called 'evaluation apprehension,' which is just a fancy way of saying people care more when they know they are being singled out. Their anxiety levels decrease when they know their effort will be pooled with others. People relax. People coast.

<u>Group Limitations</u> (Dumbars' Number)

Dumbar's number is a limitation on the number of people in groups. People can maintain relationships and keep up with only around 150 people at once. It isn't true that there is an index card in every people's mind with the names and faces of everyone people have ever known. [McRaney 2011]

Are there any natural limitations regarding the number of personal relations people can maintain during their life? The human brain, being an immense biological machine, is capable of storing all the information of people's relationships over their lifetime. For some, it is possible to affirm there is an index card in every people's mind with the names and faces of everyone they have ever known. The problem is not the space to store the information in the brain, it is the amount of energy required to maintain that information that causes the limitation.

In other primates, social relationships are maintained by grooming – picking bugs off of one another. Getting together for any reason is still a grooming behavior. People hang out, work on projects, and talk on the phone to keep connected. As technology has allowed people to be farther and farther apart yet still keep in touch with loved ones, their grooming behavior has remained constant.

Modern humans are deeply interconnected. But people can't keep up with all those other people and their connections. Internet social networks with hundreds of people sharing status updates, corporations with branches around the world – our brain is incapable of handling the multitude of human contacts populating these examples. All those personalities and quirks, the history of your interactions with each, it becomes a giant file of social information that takes constant maintenance.

The complexity of relationships builds exponentially with each new member. There is a maximum amount of time and effort people can spend – the zero-sum system. According to Dunbar, the larger the group, the more time must be spent by each member to maintain social cohesion.

Dunbar's number explains why big groups are made of smaller, more manageable groups like companies, platoons, and squads – or branches, divisions, departments, and committees. No human institution can efficiently function above 150 members without hierarchies, ranks, roles, and divisions.

Chapter 4: Human Values

People have their own set of values, and there is no objective fact about which set is best. ... there is no cosmic 'right' or 'wrong' here. ... Nietzsche has a lot to say – indeed, many volumes! - about what is good and noble for human beings, and about what is sick, weak, and despicable. There are indeed facts about these values. His claim is only that the traditional assignment of values – particularly over what is 'good' or 'evil' – is a huge mistake, grounded in a hopelessly inadequate understanding of reality. [Huenemann 2009]

Equality, rights, obligations and, agreements, among others, are considered universal drivers. Each society can add new principles adapted to its particularities. Citizens are in charge of acknowledging the set of principles that apply to particular situations. The peculiar force of morality and the sense of duty set us outside and against the order of nature. We are law-governed creatures, and even when we defy the law, we act on the assumption that we are subject to nonnegotiable demands – reasons that have the power to silence countervailing considerations, however closely they represent our empirical interests. [Scruton 2017]

Humans believe in principles that are independent of political systems and politics must be influenced by the needs of humans. Some important human principles include equality, freedom, free will, and social justice. Politicians, if they want to remain important in the future, should take into consideration most human principles to define alternative ideologies. Principles are truths or propositions invented by humans to define the foundation for a system of beliefs and behaviors to justify a chain of reasoning. Human rights are principles that any political system should be pursuing.

This new naturalism point of view, driven by biology and other sciences, generates two great spiritual dilemmas. The first is that no species, ours included, possesses a purpose beyond the imperatives created by its genetic history. The first dilemma, in a word, is that we have no particular place to go or objective to pursue. The species lacks any goal external to its biological nature. Educated people everywhere like to believe that beyond material needs lie fulfillment and the realization of individual potential. But what is fulfillment, and to what ends may potential be realized?

For humans, it is an advantage not to have a unique purpose in life. It means people are free to define their path in life, different from other people. The problem is that most people tend to imitate other people and it takes longer to become who they are. To find out who people are they need to understand their strengths and weaknesses and define their beliefs and desires in life.

The second dilemma answers the conscious choices that must be made among the ethical premises, inherent in man's biological nature, among our innate mental propensities. There are innate censors and motivators in the brain that deeply and unconsciously affect our ethical premises; from these roots, morality evolved as instinct. Which of the censors and motivators should be obeyed and which ones might better be curtailed or sublimated? [Wilson 1978]

Humans have inherent limitations that make them behave in different ways under varied circumstances. Humans have some predisposition to morality that is not absolutely shared by all. The diversity is so powerful that humans can change their minds over time. Ideologies should not be static projections over time, flexibility must be part of the equation of ideological reasoning.

Humanism

Humanism is a philosophy of life oriented to the fulfillment of human needs and interests through a more humane and compassionate society. It promotes liberty and opportunity, facilitating social justice and protecting the dignity of individuals. It is based on naturalism and rejects supernatural beliefs such as unreal theological convictions. Humanists affirm that humans have the freedom to give meaning, value, and purpose to their lives by their independent thought, free inquiry, and responsible, creative activity. Human reasoning, experience, and knowledge are sustained by science and pragmatic ethics judging the consequences of actions by the well-being of humans and other species on Earth and the universe. Human right is an important component of humanism.

Individuality

Most people, especially those in Western cultures, like to see themselves as individuals, as people who march to a different beat. Most people are probably the same sort of person who values their identity. Individuality is related to the quality or character of a particular person or thing that distinguishes them from others of the same kind; being a person separated from other people and possessing their own needs or goals, rights, and responsibilities.

Equality

According to biology, humans were not created, they have evolved. And they certainly did not evolve to be 'equal'. The idea of equality is inextricably intertwined with the idea of creation. The Americans got the idea of equality from Christianity, which argues that every person has a divinely created soul and that all souls are equal before God. However, if we do not believe in the Christian myths about God, creation, and souls, what does it mean that all people are 'equal'? Evolution is based on differences, not on equality. Every person carries a somewhat different genetic code and is exposed from birth to different environmental influences. This leads to the development of different qualities that carry with them different chances of survival. 'Created equal' should, therefore, be translated into 'evolved differently'. [Harari 2014]

What kind of equality are we talking about? A fair approach would be equality equivalent to opportunity. Everybody having equal opportunities to demonstrate their capacities. Those more capable get the chance to excel and keep ahead, the rest stay behind. Are men equal to women or blacks equal to whites? Physically they are different, there is no choice, blacks have pigmentation that whites don't; women and men differ on gender. However, having equal opportunities according to skills is an excellent equality proposition; give opportunities to blacks, whites, men, and women. The same analysis applies to other contexts either physical or mental: skilled and unskilled, good and evil, smart and dumb, beautiful and ugly, and so on. We must be precise about what equality means.

Equality has always been the most important principle dreamed by intellectuals. Equality should be referred primarily to educational, social or collaborative types of equality because intellectual and physical equality is unattainable. Economic equality is also an objective although subject to the effort of each individual. Treating everybody according to the same economic parameters alienates individuals; better economic conditions represent an independent measurement of success.

Both the Code of Hammurabi and the American Declaration of Independence claim to outline universal and eternal principles of justice, but according to the Americans, all people are equal, whereas according to the Babylonians people are decidedly unequal. The two texts present us with an obvious dilemma. The Americans would, of course, say that they are right and that Hammurabi is wrong. Hammurabi, naturally, would retort that he is right and that the Americans are wrong. They are both wrong. Hammurabi and the American Founding Fathers alike imagined a reality governed by universal and immutable principles of justice, such as equality or hierarchy. Yet the only place where such universal principles exist is in the fertile imagination of Sapiens through the myths they invent and tell one another. And these principles have no objective validity. [Harari 2014]

Advocates of equality and human rights may be outraged by this type of reasoning. Their response is likely to be, 'We know that people are not equal biologically! But if we believe that we are all equal, it will enable us to create a stable and prosperous society.' There is no argument with that. This is exactly what it is meant by 'imagined order'. We believe in a particular order not because it is objectively true, but because believing in it enables us to cooperate effectively and forge a better society. Imagined orders are not evil conspiracies or useless mirages. Rather, they are the only way large numbers of humans can cooperate effectively. Bear in mind, though, that Hammurabi might have defended his principle of hierarchy using the same logic: 'I know that superiors, commoners, and slaves are not inherently different kinds of people. But if we believe that they are, it will enable us to create a stable and prosperous society.' [Harari 2014]

Nietzsche gave a discourse on the notion of equality, 'In Thus Spoke Zarathustra,' Part 2, (7) The Tarantulas, "Revenge is in your soul: wherever you bite, there arises black scab; with revenge, your poison makes the soul giddy! Thus do I speak to you in a parable, you who make the soul giddy, you preachers of equality! Tarantulas are you to me, and secretly revengeful ones! Therefore do I tear at your web, that your rage may lure you out of your den of lies, and that your revenge may leap forth from behind your word 'justice.' 'Vengeance will we use, and insult, against all who are not like us' - thus do the tarantula-hearts pledge themselves. And 'Will to Equality' – that itself shall henceforth be the name of virtue; and against all that has power will we raise an outcry!" [Nietzsche 2003]

Free will

The great paradox between determinism and free will can be phrased as follows: if our genes are inherited and our environment is a train of physical events set in motion before we were born, how can there be a truly independent agent within the brain? The agent itself is created by the interaction of the genes and the environment. It would appear that our freedom is only a self-delusion. [Wilson 1978]

Free will is a valued principle for humans. Humans are autonomous entities with the capability to accept or reject the imposition of the state or any other authority figure. As a self-conscious subject, I have a point of view on the world. The world seems a certain way to me, and this "seeming" defines my unique perspective. Every self-conscious being has such a perspective since that is what it means to be a subject of consciousness. [Scruton 2017]

Free will is the power of acting without the constraint of necessity or fate; the ability to act at one's discretion. Free will is closely linked to the concepts of responsibility, praise, guilt, sin, and other judgments that apply only to actions that are freely chosen.

Freedom

Freedom is a valued principle for humans, it stands for something greater than just the right to act however we choose; it includes, among others, the absence of a despotic government. Free speech, free assembly, and free enterprise are some of the most looked after values. Freedom also stands for securing to everyone an equal opportunity for life, liberty, and the pursuit of happiness. Humans deserve freedom although with some limitations regarding coexistence with other fellow humans.

Social Justice

There is a relationship among the concepts of morality, politics, and philosophy that must be taken into consideration when defining social justice. Current political philosophy explores the virtues of a benevolent state and usually makes social justice, sometimes liberty, into the overarching aim of government. The critical instruments of social coordination are the system of rights and duties (morality), the virtues that motivate us to obey it, and the political backing that makes obedience possible and which coordinates our many and diverse interests. [Scruton 2017]

Virtues

Ancient thinkers distinguished four cardinal virtues – courage, prudence, temperance, and justice – and vice was its opposite. Virtues are dispositions that we praise, and their absence is an object of shame. It is through virtue that our actions and emotions remain centered in the self, and vice means the decentering of action and emotion so that the I and its undertakings no longer have a place in determining what one feels and does. Vice is a loss of self-control and the vicious person is the one on whom we cannot rely on matters of obligation and commitment. [Scruton 2017]

Virtues are human characteristics that require constant support. Aristotle's virtue consisted of the ability to pursue what reason recommends, despite the motives that strive against it. It consists of the ability to take full responsibility for one's acts. Intentions, and avowals, in the face of all motives for renouncing or denouncing them... we are human beings, with animal fears and appetites, and not transcendental subjects, motivated by reason alone. [Scruton 2017]

The virtues of Anglo-Saxons are independence and self-reliance, individual initiative and local responsibility, the successful reliance on voluntary activity, noninterference with one's neighbor and tolerance of the different and queer, respect for custom and tradition, and a healthy suspicion of power and authority. [Hayek 1994]

Nobility is related to virtue, even though it was associated with a social class during the Middle Ages. Today, nobility should be associated with the characteristics of people who have high morals and ideals, and who are always honest and charitable. Nietzsche was one who used the term most frequently to emphasize high personal qualities. Pursuing nobility means developing the courage to push yourself beyond anywhere you expected to be. It is anything but rest, peace, and complacency. It is an aggressive drive into enemy territory, welcoming every painful injury as a friend, as an encouragement to further growth. [Huenemann 2009]

Industriousness

Average people spend a great deal of time waiting for things to happen, they don't establish goals in their life. They make countless excuses to postpone taking action and are distracted all the time. People with goals, on the other hand, constantly do something and try new stuff to move forward. This way, creating opportunities and making the most of them is part of working hard. Hard work gives people a purpose, it helps them overcome laziness, procrastination, doubts, fear of failure, insecurities, and bad habits.

The best measure for anything is progress. And there's nothing else that brings more results consistently than hard work. What's more, the action itself leads to more action and at any moment of the day, people are building momentum and making sure their journey continues. A universal law is that the more people are focused on something and take action connected to it, the more doors are open and the more life gives them chances to get closer to their vision.

Getting results makes people feel accomplished, grateful and truly satisfied with what they're doing. It makes the whole process enjoyable and they must find the strength to persevere, to take action instead of waiting for things to happen, to stop blaming others, and to take responsibility for anything they have done or not in their job.

It doesn't matter who the workers are, what they do, or whom they work with, workers must be accountable. They must be responsible for their tasks, and accountable for all that they do and don't. Working on goals is the motivation people need to keep moving forward and say no to distractions from daily life. People need to be patient, and to appreciate all they have but still aim higher.

Effective interpersonal skills are crucial for any worker. Period. If a worker wants to be effective and efficient, she needs to have good listening and communication skills to be able to develop relationships that can promote organizational objectives. Good interpersonal skills allow people to get what they want, whenever they want, wherever they need it from.

When a worker has a task to do, people want it to get done and get done well. There's a reason to delegate tasks, the job has to be completed without having to worry about it. What people don't want is having that worker ask a million questions! This is why being resourceful is one of the most important qualities of a good worker.

Two heads are better than one – it's as simple as that! A great quality of a worker is his willingness to open up and share his ideas and experiences. After all, it's our past experiences that have taught us all we know, and if workers are willing to share that knowledge then everyone is benefiting.

Optimism and Pessimism

What should be the correct attitude to life knowing that the human condition has no specific purpose by itself? It would be reckless to choose the worse alternative having so many possibilities of enjoying an interesting life. Optimism and pessimism are always present in humans. There is an optimistic attitude to life in which people are confident that they can readily solve any problems they come across. They use to show courage, openness, frankness, responsibility, hard work, and so on. The opposite of this is pessimism: timidity, introspection, and distrust which are characteristics of weakling entities.

As an academic definition, optimism and pessimism can help identify personality tendencies, therefore they are modeling tools, but in practice, people are much more complex than that. Putting optimism and pessimism as black and white choices is unfair to humans. Every human being can go through periods of optimism and pessimism. These characteristics are related to a personality trait that defines our tendency toward one or the other during all our life. A weakling personality can be pessimistic and still be a responsible and hard worker, thus contributing to society.

There is one type of human being who always overvalues other's personal opinions and therefore undervalues their own, whether they are right or wrong; it is a trait related to self-esteem. A second type sees every stimulus or suggestion as an insult. These are individuals who consider that only their own opinion is right. Both types carry with them a sense of weakness. New generations do not necessarily show greater improvements compared to their ancestors; war is a clear example of our innate difficulties to find solutions to common problems. [Adler 1992]

Tolerance

The largest sources of discrimination in humanity came from religious misguidance and political wrongdoing. Many battles have been fought in the name of God or the homeland. Tolerance was not the supreme criterion to avoid bloodshed. Uncomprehending is a normal attitude in humans. Human nature makes us potentially intolerant. It is difficult to get rid of that characteristic. Some say education should help to combat these defects but most of the time we have to accept imperfections. [Adler 1992]

Tolerance is the ability or willingness to accept something that we do not necessarily agree with, in particular, the expression of opinions or behaviors that collides with our own. Human beings have been persistent on discrimination and bigotry; the unjust or prejudicial treatment of different categories of people or things, especially on the grounds of race, age, sex, or ideology, and the intolerance toward those who hold different opinions from ourselves.

Forgiveness

Forgiveness means to stop blaming or being angry with someone for something that person has done, or not punishing him for something. It does not mean forgetting, nor does it means condoning or excusing offenses. Forgiveness cannot be offered arbitrarily and to all comers – so offered it becomes a kind of indifference, a refusal to recognize the distinction between right and wrong. Forgiveness is only sincerely offered by a person who is aware of having been wronged, to another who is aware of having committed a wrong. [Scruton 2017]

Animals use to have a better approach to forgiveness. Most of the time they just want to stay alive and avoid trouble. Humans are more resentful, they do not forget and keep fighting back for long periods.

Part II: Behavioral Framework

Human behavior is first and foremost a kind of "doing" or "acting" according to specific interests or motivators. Individuals do what they do because of either implicit or explicit ethical or practical (including economic cost-benefit) analyses to produce certain outcomes. When we try to understand people's behavior and explain why they do what they do, what framework do we use? One alternative is to use a framework of motivators, actions, personal and social influences and the justifications supporting these elements.

Human behavior is directed by interests or motivators to start actions or work efforts to produce change or satisfaction. As persons, we have specific characteristics originated initially by genetics and transformed by our interaction with the environment. The social environment influences our actions and might impact others or define how the actions themselves might be shaped by social factors. Finally, there is the explanatory system that people use to make sense of the world around them and legitimize what they are doing and why.

Motivators

The most common, intuitive approach to establish the motivators of human behavior is the "belief-desire-needs" trilogy. That is, people in everyday situations use beliefs, desires, and needs to explain why they do what they do. Evolution has primed us to value certain states of affairs (e.g., safety, territory, food, sex, higher social status) over others. And, of course, our learning history directly shapes our motivational value system.

Doing or Acting

Work efforts, which involve several possible considerations, include among others, productive, spiritual and recreational activities. Specific outcomes are guided by expected time and effort, reward objectives, opportunity analysis, costs, risks, and so forth.

Personal Influences

People differ in terms of temperaments and dispositions, much of which is strongly influenced by genetics. For example, extroverted people find stimulating social situations more rewarding than introverted people.

Social Influences

We are incredibly social animals, and one of the most important features around our environment is other people. And our actions rarely take place in isolation, but they take place in the context of a social environment. Important social influence processes involve competition, cooperation, and social exchanges to move people closer (i.e., become more dependent) or to move them further apart (become more independent).

Social influence refers to two things. The first meaning is the process by which one person's actions impact the actions of another person and it is related to the capacity to move other people following one's interests. The second meaning interprets influence as a resource. It refers to the levels of respect and social value other people show us, the extent to which they listen, care about our well-being and are willing to sacrifice for us.

Justification

"Justification" is a broad concept that refers to both the systematic structure and the legitimizing function of verbal communication (including reading and writing). Justification can be thought of as anything that involves questions and answers which lead to claims about what is and what ought to be. Arguments, reasons for and against things, rationalizations, laws, and even scientific truth claims, all are "justifications." Justifications abound, why are we motivated? Why do we do what we do? what influence has the person? What influence has the society?

Chapter 5: Life Motivators

People think they know how the world around them works but in reality, they don't. People have no clue why they act the way they do, choose the things they choose or think the thoughts they think; people create narratives to explain the way they behave. They live an illusion that seems real and where the main character is the individual and its surroundings. To compensate for this lack of knowledge, people define life motivators based on beliefs, desires, and needs. For example, why do they follow a diet (to live healthy, to keep a nice body), why do they prefer a certain car model (to spend less on gas, to look important), why do they admire a populist politician (to help the poor, to feel justice is done), and so on. Thanks to their ability to invent fiction, Sapiens created more and more complex games of life. The historical evolution of their actions determines the understanding of their behavior. [Harari 2014]

People invent stories reflecting their understanding of life and they choose among alternatives after conflicting arguments inside their minds. The brain and the nervous system drive people's behavior letting them survive and thrive. They invent stories and run imagined and remembered events back and forth through time: destroying enemies, embracing lovers, carving tools from blocks of steel, traveling easily into the realms of myth and perfection. They form opinions and cobble together stories about who they are and why they did things the way they did. Maslow's theory of motivation is a good starting point that identifies many of the factors that motivate human behavior.

Needs, Beliefs, and Desires

Maslow's hierarchy of needs offers an alternative to what other psychologists, such as Freud and Skinner, established as depressing determinism. Maslow called attention to the differences between his optimistic view and the other's denial of human freedom and dignity. Lying, cheating, stealing, and murder are not what he thought human nature was meant to be.

Think of someone who fits the following description: loving, fair, realistic, relaxed, self-sufficient, spontaneous, creative, nice. This is the kind of extraordinary person Abraham Maslow considered when he devised a theory of motivation fifty years ago. Make sure he or she also has an honest directness, a playful spirit, a history of successful risk-taking, and a way of moving through life that seems effortless. [Maslow 1970]

The most basic drives are physiological. Next comes the need for safety, then the desire for love, and then the quest for esteem. Maslow referred to these needs as "deficiency needs" because their lack creates a tension within us. As long as we can work to satisfy the cravings, we're moving toward growth. Satisfying needs is healthy. Blocking gratification makes us sick. Finally, the need for self-actualization is the endeavor that makes us more proficient in our actions.

Physiological Needs

Physiological needs are basic: The body craves for food, liquid, sleep, oxygen, sex, freedom of movement, and moderate temperature. When any of these are in short supply, we feel the distressing tension of hunger, thirst, fatigue, shortness of breath, sexual frustration, confinement, or the discomfort of being too hot or too cold.

Safety Needs

The safety needs operate mainly on a psychological level. Political appeals for law and order are aimed at people whose insecurities have never been quieted. Maslow also placed religious inclination on the safety rung because he saw that tendency as an attempt to bring about an ordered universe with no nasty shocks. We may categorize roughly as the safety needs: security; stability; dependency; protection; freedom from fear, from anxiety and chaos; the need for structure, order, law, limits; strength in the protector; and so on.

Love and Belonging Needs

People will hunger for affectionate relations with other people in general, namely, for a place in his group or family, and they will strive with great intensity to achieve this goal. Gratification is a matter of degree rather than an either-or accomplishment. Maslow's concept of belonging combines the twin urges to give and receive love. For Maslow, giving love is seeking to fill a void by understanding and accepting selected others. Receiving love is a way of staving off the pangs of loneliness and rejection.

Esteem Needs

All people in our society (with a few pathological exceptions) have a need or desire for a stable, firmly based, usually high evaluation of themselves, for self-respect, or self-esteem, and the esteem of others. The satisfaction of self-esteem need leads to feelings of self-confidence, worth, strength, capability, and adequacy, of being useful and necessary in the world. But thwarting of these needs produces feelings of inferiority, of weakness, and helplessness.

The esteem needs are of two types. There's self-esteem, which is the result of competence or mastery of tasks. Psychologists call this "need for achievement." There's also the attention and recognition that come from others. Wanting this admiration is part of what psychologists label "need for power."

These are, first, the desire for strength, for achievement, for adequacy, for mastery and competence, for confidence in the face of the world, and independence and freedom. Second, people have what they may call the desire for reputation or prestige (defining it as respect or esteem from other people), status, fame and glory, dominance, recognition, attention, importance, dignity, or appreciation.

Self-actualization: The Ultimate Goal

Maslow described the need for self-actualization as "the desire to become more and more what one is, to become everything that one is capable of becoming" Self-actualization can take many forms, depending on the individual. These variations may include the quest for knowledge, understanding, peace, self-fulfillment, meaning in life, or beauty.

It refers to people's desire for self-fulfillment, namely, the tendency to become actualized in what they are potentially proficient. This tendency might be phrased as the desire to become more and more what one idiosyncratically is, to become everything that one is capable of becoming.

Maslow's theory of motivation does have a healthy emphasis on freedom of choice. He believes that the ability to respond is what makes us fully human. With this in mind, one might wish that he had placed more emphasis on responsible, unselfish commitment to others.

Beliefs

Beliefs are our brain's way of making sense of and navigating through our complex world. They are mental representations of the ways our brains expect things in our environment to behave, and how things should be related to each other – the patterns our brain expects the world to conform to. Beliefs are templates for efficient learning and are often essential for survival.

The brain is an energy-expensive organ, so it had to evolve energy-conserving efficiencies. As a prediction machine, it must take shortcuts for pattern recognition as it processes the vast amounts of information received from the environment by its senses. Beliefs allow the brain to distill complex information, enabling it to quickly categorize and evaluate information and to jump to conclusions.

These shortcuts to interpreting and predicting our world often involve connecting dots and filling in gaps, making extrapolations and assumptions based on incomplete information and based on similarity to previously recognized patterns. In jumping to conclusions, our brains have a preference for familiar conclusions over unfamiliar ones. Thus, our brains are prone to error, sometimes seeing patterns where there are none. This may or may not be subsequently identified and corrected by error-detection mechanisms. It's a trade-off between efficiency and accuracy.

In its need for economy and efficiency of energy consumption, the default tendency of the brain is to fit new information into its existing framework for understanding the world, rather than repeatedly reconstructing that framework from scratch.

It's not surprising that our brains have evolved to more readily believe things told to us than to be skeptical. This makes evolutionary sense as a strategy for efficient learning from parents, and as a social, tribal species it promotes group cohesion. A lot of our belief framework is learned at an early age from parents and other adult authority figures. Children are strongly predisposed to believe their parents, and, as adults, we are inclined to believe authorities. Many human beliefs are the cumulative chain of millennia of human culture.

People can be swayed by persuasive individuals or compelling ideas to override and reject their previously received ideas from another authority. Sometimes, this is rational. But sometimes, it is not – people are susceptible to influence by charismatic ideologues and by social movements. Especially when these offer new attachments and new self-identities imbued with more powerful affiliation, validation, esteem and sense of purpose than the individual previously had in his or her life.

Desires

Desire is intimately connected to pleasure and pain. Human beings feel pleasure at the things that, in the course of their evolution, have tended to promote their survival and reproduction; they feel pain at the things that have tended to compromise their genes. The pleasurable things, such as sugar, sex, and social status, are wired to be desirable, whereas the painful things, such as illness, isolation, and hard work are wired to be undesirable.

Moreover, as soon as a desire is fulfilled, people stop taking pleasure in its fulfillment and instead formulate new desires, because, in the course of evolution, contentedness and complacency did not tend to promote survival and reproduction.

Our intellect, in which we place so much faith, evolved to assist us in our pursuit of the desirable and avoidance of the undesirable. It did not evolve to enable us to resist our desires, still less to transcend them. Although our intellect is subservient to our desires, it is good at fooling us that it is in control.

Desires can be divided into natural and unnatural desires. Natural desires such as those for food and shelter are naturally limited. In contrast, unnatural or vain desires such as those for fame, power, or wealth are potentially unlimited. Unnatural desires, which are unlimited, have their roots not in nature but society. All these desires can be understood in terms of social status. Indeed, were we to be the last person on earth, being famous, powerful, or wealthy would not only be of no use but would be meaningless.

The society also gives rise to destructive desires such as the desire to make others envy us, or the desire to see others fail, or, at least, not succeed as much as us. We suffer not only from our destructive desires but also from the destructive desires of others, turning into the target and victim of their insecurities.

Self-control

Self-control is related to desires as a way of controlling the forces that drive humanity. It is the ability to control ourselves, in particular, our emotions and desires or the expression of them through our behavior, especially in difficult situations.

Have you ever had a car accident while approaching a transit intersection when a yellow light has turned on? In many cases, drivers increase the speed instead of slowing down, facilitating the possibility of an accident. Have you, in that situation, ever been crossed by a car in the middle of the intersection? This is a scary incident, and a way to avoid it is by exercising a preventive action. Self-control would mean slowing a bit down before the intersection, while the light is still green, instead of increasing the speed. One way to overcome many dangers is to prevent them to happen. Self-control is a learned behavior that can keep us alive. This recommendation can be considered a responsive self-control attitude.

Additional Motivators

Among other motivators for human behavior, let us present some factors and principles that determine the decision making processes that favor a certain action over another. Principles such as equality, free will, freedom, and social justice involve cultural drivers. Factors such as intentions, interests, illusions, and suffering are related to the individual and its surroundings.

Most people have no goal in their life, they live like cattle grazing the grass. However, people must define some goals to thrive for in a society; a politician must define goals to improve his society; an athlete must define goals to progress in her sports; a student must define goals to become a professional; an artist must define goals to improve her work of art. Surviving should not be a goal by itself because everybody must survive, instead, it should be considered an automatic life-saving mechanism.

Intentions

What is the prime mover, the weaver who guides the human experience? Cognitive psychologists suggest humans are motivated by intentionality, which is related to a schema or plan. Intentionality is the cardinal mystery of neurobiology. Human beings are "intentional systems" - organisms that exhibit intentional states that are systematically connected.

An intention is not the same thing as a desire: people can intend to do what they don't want to do and want to do what they don't intend to do. Intending something means being certain that you will do it and also knowing why. Intending is not predicting. I predict that I won't eat chocolate tonight, but maybe I'll grab a byte just for gluttony. [Scruton 2017]

Interests

Interest is a preference for one activity over another. The selection and ranking of different activities along a like – dislike dimension is known as expressed interest. Interest is made manifest (visible) when a person voluntarily participates in an activity.

There is not necessarily a relationship between expressed interest and manifest interest, though in many situations they tend to coincide or overlap. Many individuals engage in some activities which they claim to dislike and just on the reverse, many people may refuse to engage in activities which they claim to enjoy.

Illusions

Evolution provided pleasant feelings as rewards to males who spread their genes by having sex with fertile females. If sex were not accompanied by such pleasure, few males would bother. At the same time, evolution made sure that these pleasant feelings quickly subsided. If orgasms were to last forever, the very happy males would die of hunger for lack of interest in food, and would not take the trouble to look for additional fertile females. [Harari 2014]

Think for a moment of your family and friends. You know some people who remain relatively joyful, no matter what befalls them. And then some are always disgruntled, no matter what gifts the world lays at their feet. We tend to believe that if we could just change our workplace, get married, finish writing that novel, buy a new car or repay the mortgage, we would be on top of the world. Yet when we get what we desire we don't seem to be any happier. Buying cars and writing novels do not change our biochemistry. They can startle it for a fleeting moment, but it is soon back to its set point. [Harari 2014]

How can this be squared with some psychological and sociological findings that, for example, married people are happier on average than singles? First, these findings are correlations – the direction of causation may be the opposite of what some researchers have assumed. Married people are indeed happier than singles and divorcees, but that does not necessarily mean that marriage produces happiness. It could be that happiness causes marriage. Or more correctly, that serotonin, dopamine, and oxytocin bring about and maintain a marriage. People who are born with cheerful biochemistry are generally happy and content. Such people are more attractive spouses, and consequently, they have a greater chance of getting married. They are also less likely to divorce because it is far easier to live with a happy and content spouse than with a depressed and dissatisfied one. Consequently, married people are indeed happier on average than singles, but a single woman prone to gloom because of her biochemistry would not necessarily become happier if she were to hook up with a husband. [Harari 2014]

The illusory nature of pleasure means that you would not believe that there is any reason to aim at it. What you want is the reality of a successful career, loving marriage, and so on, and the illusion is not a second-best but something that is not rational to want at all. [Scruton 2017]

Suffering

Suffering is one of the big motivators for things we do on earth. There are various sources and kinds of suffering, physical (pain, somatic diseases), psychical (hardships, mental disorders, and illnesses) and spiritual (lack of a meaningful life, moral dilemmas). Psychic suffering is a correlative between both mental and spiritual sufferings.

Suffering fulfills a variety of functions in the life and personality of a human being; it can cause a personality degradation or can further personality development. Therefore, we can speak of the ambivalent character of suffering.

The elementary psychological problem, encountered in suffering, is to give suffering some meaning. To do this one must ask about the future: for whom and what do I suffer? Knowing about the ultimate origin of suffering, why do I suffer? not only makes it possible to explain the issue fully but first of all, allows us to recognize suffering as a mystery of human existence.

Political and economic situations make people suffer by reducing the possibilities of decent survival in societies. Even if we have not endured post-traumatic stress, we are all familiar with hardship. Some people go through poverty or abuse. Others withstand bullying, breakups, or illness. Suffering is universal, albeit manifested in different ways and to different extents.

Chapter 6: Doing or Acting

"'Become who you are!' is Nietzsche's recurring injunction, but of course it does not mean resting comfortably with whatever you find yourself to be. It somehow is meant to connote striving, struggle, stripping away, discovering to terms with, and amplifying. Becoming who you are is an ongoing, unending process aimed at a higher altitude, finding more and more beneath oneself, finding contentment only at summits and glaciers:..." [Huenemann 2009]

Some people do not understand themselves. Some undervalue themselves, and still, others are not sufficiently aware of their shortcomings. It does not matter what you think of yourself, or what other people think of you. The important thing is the general attitude towards society since this determines every wish, every interest and every activity of each individual. [Adler 1992]

In the Gay Science (284 Belief in Oneself), Nietzsche expresses the need for believing in yourself and trying to go beyond the surface:

"In general, few men have belief in themselves: - and of those few, some are endowed with it as useful blindness or partial obscuration of intellect (what would they perceive if they could see to the bottom of themselves)." [Chapko 2010]

<u>Active Life</u>

It is difficult to know ourselves and the worst way is to stay inactive. If people are passive, they will wish only to accept their limitations, their charming quirks, and foibles, and conclude that they are happy with who they are. But if they are active, they will not let themselves rest so easily. They are more than this. They have not yet discovered the strength at their command. They do not yet know who or what they are. Only by welcoming sharp adversity will they ever begin to discover their mettle. [Huenemann 2009]

In the Gay Science (297 Ability to Contradict), Nietzsche expresses the need to contradict, hopefully when it is worth to do it:

"Everyone knows at present that the ability, to endure contradiction is a good indication of culture. Some people even know that the higher man courts opposition, and provokes it, to get a cue to his until now unknown partiality. But the ability to contradict, ... is the great, new and astonishing thing in our culture, the step of all steps of the emancipated intellect: who knows that?" [Chapko 2010]

Will to Power

The will to power is an abstraction that may mean many different things. It is one of those concepts that Nietzsche wanted to retain undisturbed and unclear. The will to power, the will to love, the will to justice, the will to knowledge, and so on, are ways of stressing action, the need to perform instead of staying passive. In society several entities play a role in converting passivity into action. For example, government institutions, clubs, families, are places where action makes a difference, compared to apathy.

The will to power can be interpreted as the will to be in power, to command, to control the life of everybody. However, it is a more subtle concept. It is oriented to be active, to take a position, to challenge old ideas, and so on. Nietzsche was planning to write a book about that subject, but in the end, he had no time. However, some notes were published by his sister. For example, Zarathustra declares: "Wherever I found living things, I found the will to power." The doctrine of the "will to power," as delineated in Thus Spoke Zarathustra, consists primarily of the principle of self-transcendence. The will to power is first and foremost the will to power over oneself. [Nietzsche 2003]

Power exists if it is considered useful, following the criteria of the interested party. Of course, the power of one person becomes concrete in the imagination of another. Nietzsche realized at an early stage that power is not just agonizing but also imaginative, not substantive but relational. It exists only concerning how is regarded, which means that we need to move away from a mechanistic model with a material basis.

Financial income is not the only type of interest, there are other types of interests such as love and justice, for example. If power relations are inextricably linked to the powers of imagination of all parties involved, the imagination is part of the process of outpouring the innermost power from one human being to another.

Power can be attached to individuals and groups. A powerful individual is powerful only to the extent that it appears strong, valuable, smart, essential, indispensable, unconquerable, to others. States, organizations, and families are examples of groups that exercise power within and without. The state is one of the more dangerous power groups because its decisions affect the whole population. Take also the case of the

United Nations, a group, which may affect some countries that do not comply with their mandates.

Zarathustra comes down to the individual when talking about the will to power. It sounds interesting. It is not only the power to command others but primarily the power to control yourself. It is oriented to change apathy and to become engaged. Many people are obedient and submissive, letting others take charge. Better let your opinion count and play an active role. [Nietzsche 2003]

In Safranski, inversion and self-referentiality are characteristics for both Nietzsche and Zarathustra. Our attention is shifted from the object of an intention to the intentional act. The "will to ..." is brought into focus. [Safranski 2002]

The most common form of a group is the family and everybody is aware of the power struggles within it. Take the case of parents that do not agree on many subjects and must find ways to reconcile differences. Most of the time, wives accept the power of the husband because he is the one providing economic security for the family. Therefore it is not precisely reasoning involved in but, let us exaggerate, brute force. Many relationships are based on supposed power from one of the partners over the other. Sometimes, kids believe that one parent has the power and the other is just an object being manipulated by that powerful partner; reasoning does not enter into their equation either, kids manipulate the powerful parent to obtain their desires.

Referring to Safranski on the subject of life. Life aspires to itself and strives to configure itself, but consciousness maintains an ambivalent relationship with this principle of self-configuration of living things. Consciousness can act as an inhibiting or an enhancing force. It can elicit anxieties, moral scruples, and resignation, and can cause the vital impulses to snap, but consciousness can also place itself in the service of life by pronouncing valuations that encourage life to engage in a free activity, refinement, and sublimation. [Safranski 2002]

Who is going to disagree with Nietzsche on this? People would like to do whatever they want without worrying about anything. However, consciousness brings up the best in humans, making them free thinkers and actors that can transform the world. Life may be seen as a matter of common sense or a Dionysian vision of life. Remind you that Dionysian is usually a chaotic point of view.

Societies cannot accept a Dionysian vision of life, maybe some small groups can follow that path under scrutiny. Provided that groups do not interfere with the rest of society, their behavior might be tolerated, but most of the time there are conflicts among groups. Remind you that in our society, laws are made to simplify procedures, therefore most people are unsatisfied with those laws.

Some religions try to limit the liberty of individuals by prohibiting sins through their commandments. If people followed only Dionysian irrationality and chaos, fueled only by emotions and instincts, probably our society would not progress as expected. Apollonian suggestions of rational thinking and order, appealing to prudence and purity, are followed by many societies. As usual, it is better not to generalize, a good mix of both philosophies is the recipe human beings must follow, everything is not only work and everything is not only fun.

The sociopolitical world of the foragers is another area about which we know next to nothing. It is not known whether private property, nuclear families and monogamous relationships existed. Different bands likely had different structures. Some may have been hierarchical, tense and nastiest, while others were laid-back, peaceful and lascivious. [Harari 2014]

Chapter 7: Personal Influence

Everything around people says something about their personality. As humans, people have many similarities and at the same time many differences. Cultivating an incomparable self either through consumption or creation is not something people take lightly. People are characterized by diversity, therefore, everybody is different. The nerve system is fundamental to define people's reflexes and capacity of endurance. If variation in mental and athletic ability is influenced to a moderate degree by heredity, as the evidence suggests, we should expect individuals of truly extraordinary capacity to emerge unexpectedly in otherwise undistinguished families, and then fail to transmit these qualities to their children. [Wilson 1978]

Persons are moral beings, conscious of right and wrong, who judge their fellows and who are judged in their turn. They are primarily individuals, and any account of the moral life must begin from the apparent tension that exists between our nature as free individuals and our membership in the communities in which our fulfillment depends. [Scruton 2017]

Personality is the unique, integrated and organized system of all behavior of a person. Personality is the total sum of people's experience, thoughts, and actions; it includes all behavior patterns, traits and characteristics that make up a person. A person's physical traits, attitudes, habits and, emotional and psychological characteristics are all parts of people's personality.

Genetically influenced personality is seen clearly in the effect of physiology on physique and temperament. The role of the nervous system in the acquisition of personality traits determines their interaction. Genetic influence continues with cultural influence, commencing at birth with the infant's response to the environment and continues throughout life as the influence of the home, community and society increases during the growth and maturity of the individual. Parents, teachers, and friends exercise a great influence on the formation of attitudes and the personality as a whole. However, at the individual level, genetic influence is stronger than cultural influence.

To be a person, therefore, people must have the capacities that make relationships possible. These include self-awareness, accountability, and practical reason. Persons falling under the scope of Kant's moral law: they must respect each other as persons. In other words, they should grant each other a sphere of sovereignty. Within their sphere of sovereignty what is done, and what happens to them, insofar as it depends on human choices, depends on those choices. This can be guaranteed only if people are shielded from each other by a wall of rights and protected from aggression by a concept of desert. Without rights and deserts, individuals are not sovereigns but subjects. These rights and deserts are inherent in the condition of personhood and not derived from any convention or agreement. In other words, they are "natural." [Scruton 2017]

The abstract liberal concept of persons as centers of free choice, whose will is sovereign and whose rights determine our duties toward them, delivers only a part of moral thinking. Persons can be polluted, desecrated, defiled. As a self-conscious subject, a person has a point of view on the world. The world seems a certain way to them, and this "seeming" defines their unique perspective. Every self-conscious being has such a perspective since that is what it means to be a subject of consciousness. [Scruton 2017]

No doubt, in certain circumstances, people come to put a greater emphasis on what distinguishes them from their neighbors than on what they share; no doubt the idea of human life as a single narrative, to be understood as whole in itself, comes to the fore in some epochs and not in others; no doubt the art of some cultures celebrates individuals and their way of "standing out" from the community, while the art of other cultures looks on this posture with indifference or hostility. [Scruton 2017]

When people stand in the way of our appetites, we do not simply sweep them aside, lay hold of the prize, and ignore all rival claims to it. Should we behave in that way, then we will be greeted by hostility and resentment and threatened with punishment. The habit of blaming people arises as a natural offshoot of our competitiveness, and we respond to blame with an excuse, an apology, or an act of repentance. If none of those are forthcoming, the social conditions change. [Scruton 2017]

Those who build a universal political doctrine on the foundations of human rights require a theory that tells them which rights belong to our nature – our nature as persons – and which are the product of convention. That theory will be a theory of the person. Marxists who found their critique of bourgeois society on the idea of exploitation and the dignity of labor rely on the view that there is a fulfilled and free relation between people, which the capitalist system suppresses. That view demands a theory of the person. Theists see the goal of human life as the knowledge and love of a personal God, whose presence is revealed in the natural order. Left-liberals see political order as a mechanism for reconciling individual freedom with social justice. In every area of political conflict today we find the concept of the person at the center of the dispute yet created as a mere abstraction, with little or no attention to its social and historical context. [Scruton 2017]

First-person knowledge is peculiarly privileged – a matter not of observation but of the spontaneous ability to declare, without evidence, our beliefs, feelings, sensations, and desires. It is on this spontaneous ability that the I-You relation is built, and terms such as I and You get their sense from the resulting dialogue. But then, do they describe objects in the world of observation? Certainly, they express the point of view of the subject; but, as we have seen, subjects are not objects, and points of view are not in the world but on the world. [Scruton 2017]

Some commonly used personality types are introverts and extroverts. The introverts are people whose interests are turned inward upon themselves and their thoughts, whereas the extroverts are those whose interests are turned outward upon the environment. The introvert generally shuns social contacts and is inclined to be solitary, whereas the extrovert seeks social contacts and enjoys them. Lying in between are found people who are neither extrovert nor introvert, they are called ambiverts.

<u>Human Models</u>

There are many models to classify humans, for example dividing human beings into thinkers and doers. Thinkers are more given to meditation and reflection. They live in a world of fantasy and shun the real world. They are difficult to jolt into action. Doers reflect less, meditate hardly at all, and busy themselves with an active, matter-of-fact, down-to-earth approach to the problems of life. [Adler 1992]

Let us take the case of planners versus supervisors or laborers, the former are thinkers whilst the latter are doers. It is a mistake to believe that doers must be in charge of every activity, thinkers can collaborate in activities that require longer periods. Thinkers require a different set of skills compared with doers. It is a well-known fact that balanced groups produce better overall solutions. Put the right mix of people in a project and the results would be extraordinary.

Considerations of objectivity and subjectivity in human nature have an impact on human behavior. When people are objective, they are neutral, detached from the situation, they are not influenced by prejudices, feelings, and interests. For example, a judge would have no reason to favor the defendant or the plaintiff; a journalist would report an event without judgmental inclinations. In many cases, people do not analyze things objectively, but receive, transform and assimilate all their perceptions in the light of their conscious mind, or the depths of their unconscious mind. Subjectivity is located within people's personal feelings and opinions. People's perception is purely subjective, therefore, an effort is required to be neutral. [Adler 1992]

Personality Type Indicator (www.myersbriggs.org)

The Myers Briggs Personality Type Indicator assessment provides the characteristic ways people prefer to focus their attention, take in information, make decisions, and deal with the outer world. These preferences are grouped into four pairs of opposites and combined to form the MBTI personality type. Although people use all of these preferences at least some of the time, they naturally prefer just one in each pair. The paragraphs below summarize these preferences:

(extrovert / introvert),
(sensitive / intuitive),
(rational / emotional), and
(judging / perceiving)

Where people focus their attention

Extroversion: extroverted people tend to focus on the outer world of other people and activities.

Introversion: introverted people tend to focus on the inner world of ideas and impressions.

The way people take in information

Sensitive: sensing people tend to take in information through the five senses and focus on the here and now.

Intuitive: intuitive people tend to take in information from patterns and the big picture and focus on future possibilities.

The way people make decisions

Rational: thinking people tend to make decisions based primarily on logic and on objective analysis of cause and effect.

Emotional: feeling people tend to make decisions based primarily on values and on subjective consideration of person-centered concerns.

How people deal with the outer world

Judging: judging people tend to like a planned and organized approach to life and want to have things settled.

Perceiving: perceiving people tend to like a flexible and spontaneous approach to life and want to keep their options open.

Human Rights

Human rights have been defined to protect citizens, they are not an instrument of the state. Humans rights should be independent of political systems. Liberty, equality before the law, and private property are just a few examples of rights that are not available in socialist countries. The objective is to define universal human rights that must be implemented in any political system. There are civil, political, economic, social, cultural and collective rights.

- Civil rights (to life, liberty, and security)
- Political rights (protection of the law and equality before the law)
- Economic rights (to work, to own property and equal pay)
- Social rights (education, consenting marriage)
- Cultural rights (participation in the community)
- Collective rights (self-determination)

A simplified version of the United Nations Universal Declaration of Human Rights is presented, it was taken from the following link: **https://www.youthforhumanrights.org/what-are-human-rights/universal-declaration-of-human-rights/articles-1-15.html**

1. We Are All Born Free & Equal. We are all born free. We all have our thoughts and ideas. We should all be treated in the same way.

2. Don't Discriminate. These rights belong to everybody, whatever our differences.

3. The Right to Life. We all have the right to life, and to live in freedom and safety.

4. No Slavery. Nobody has any right to make us a slave. We cannot make anyone our slave.

5. No Torture. Nobody has any right to hurt us or to torture us.

6. You Have Rights No Matter Where You Go. I am a person just like you!

7. We're All Equal Before the Law. The law is the same for everyone. It must treat us all fairly.

8. Your Human Rights Are Protected by Law. We can all ask for the law to help us when we are not treated fairly.

9. No Unfair Detainment. Nobody has the right to put us in prison without good reason and keep us there or to send us away from our country.

10. The Right to Trial. If we are put on trial this should be in public. The people who try us should not let anyone tell them what to do.

11. We're Always Innocent Till Proven Guilty. Nobody should be blamed for doing something until it is proven. When people say we did a bad thing we have the right to show it is not true.

12. The Right to Privacy. Nobody should try to harm our good name. Nobody has the right to come into our home, open our letters, or bother us or our family without a good reason.

13. Freedom to Move. We all have the right to go where we want in our own country and to travel as we wish.

14. The Right to Seek a Safe Place to Live. If we are frightened of being badly treated in our own country, we all have the right to run away to another country to be safe.

15. Right to a Nationality. We all have the right to belong to a country.

16. Marriage and Family. Every grown-up has the right to marry and have a family if they want to. Men and women have the same rights when they are married, and when they are separated.

17. The Right to Your Own Things. Everyone has the right to own things or share them. Nobody should take our things from us without a good reason.

18. Freedom of Thought. We all have the right to believe in what we want to believe, to have a religion, or to change it if we want.

19. Freedom of Expression. We all have the right to make up our minds, to think about what we like, to say what we think, and to share our ideas with other people.

20. The Right to Public Assembly. We all have the right to meet our friends and to work together in peace to defend our rights. Nobody can make us join a group if we don't want to.

21. The Right to Democracy. We all have the right to take part in the government of our country. Every grown-up should be allowed to choose their leaders.

22. Social Security. We all have the right to affordable housing, medicine, education, and childcare, enough money to live on and medical help if we are ill or old.

23. Workers' Rights. Every grown-up has the right to do a job, to a fair wage for their work, and to join a trade union.

24. The Right to Play. We all have the right to rest from work and to relax.

25. Food and Shelter for All. We all have the right to a good life. Mothers and children, people who are old, unemployed or disabled, and all people have the right to be cared for.

26. The Right to Education. Education is a right. Primary school should be free. We should learn about the United Nations and how to get on with others. Our parents can choose what we learn.

27. Copyright. Copyright is a special law that protects one's artistic creations and writings; others cannot make copies without permission. We all have the right to our way of life and to enjoy the good things that art, science, and learning bring.

28. A Fair and Free World. There must be proper order so we can all enjoy rights and freedoms in our own country and all over the world.

29. Responsibility. We have a duty to other people, and we should protect their rights and freedoms.

30. No One Can Take Away Your Human Rights.

Chapter 8: Social Influence

Humans are imperfect. Either biologically or culturally, humans are random organisms. Humans are a bunch of improvisers that keep trying new ways of understanding life, in most cases, they fail multiple times before coming up with a good solution. The habit of blaming people arises as a natural offshoot of our competitiveness, and we respond to blame with an excuse, an apology, or an act of repentance.

Diversity

In Twilight of the Idols (Morality as Anti-nature), Nietzsche expresses clearly the principle of diversity in humans: "Finally, let's consider how naïve it is, in general, to say, 'Human beings should be such and such!' Reality shows us a captivating treasury of types, the exuberance of an evanescent play and alteration of forms. And some pathetic bystander of a moralist says to all this, 'No! Human beings should be different'? ... He even knows how human beings should be, this sanctimonious sniveler; he paints himself on the wall and pronounces, 'ecce homo!' ..." [Nietzsche 1998]

Humans have so many characteristics that their combinations can produce infinite types of variants. Taking a detailed look at the many attempts to describe some part of what is distinctive of the human condition, let us present the following sample – the use of language (Chomsky, Bennet), second-order desires (Frankfurt), second-order intentions (Grice), convention (Lewis), freedom (Kant, Sartre), self-consciousness (Kant, Fichte, Hegel), laughing and crying (Plessner), the capacity for cultural learning (Tomasello) – you will be surely persuaded that each is tracing some part of a single holistic accomplishment. [Scruton 2017]

One characteristic that distinguishes humans is that we understand things differently. We never agree in many things. Each experience has many interpretations and therefore no two people will draw the same conclusion from the same event. This accounts for the fact that we do not always learn from our experiences. Older is not always wiser! A senior citizen that never tried to improve during his life is not a good example to follow. Some seniors citizens repeat the same mistakes over and over, how are they going to help new generations? To give advise, we need privileged active minds that look always for better approaches to human behavior. It has been demonstrated that our pattern of behavior does not usually change as a result of experiences.[Adler 1992]

Obedience

Obedience is one important topic for any society. However, the obedient individuals are rendered unfit for life, because their habits of slavish obedience have left them incapable of any independent action or thought. This submissive tendency as obedient children may develop into adults that submit to any authoritative commands. [Adler 1992]

It is a pity that there are so many obedient people in the world. Sometimes, obedience is required but other times disobedience at the right time makes a difference. When a law is wrong, it must be changed, it is not acceptable to punish people under the umbrella of an insensible law.

The problem with obedience is mostly related to uncontested obedience. Any citizen should comply with the law if the law is just. However, it is the responsibility of citizens to contest unjust laws. It is in this regard that conflict arises, people bypassing the laws instead of fighting to abolish them. The first responsible entity regarding unjust laws is the state. The state is always slow to get rid of unjust laws, making citizens uncomfortable and anxious. There is a lack of appropriate communication channels, and it is not convenient to test the patience of citizens.

Contradictory though it may seem, the life of earthly servitude is, in fact, the life that God will richly reward, according to Christians. The virtuous life is the one that devalues pursuits of earthly pleasures, wealth, power, and prominence. The 'good' person is the one who subordinates all drives to serve the Church and its head, Jesus Christ. Through this servitude, the follower will raise himself higher than all earthly powers and principalities, and reap rich rewards in heaven. The servant will be the master. What feels good is bad. What feels powerful is weakness. What seems wise is folly. To live for Christ is to be dead to the world. Indeed, the very symbol of eternal life is a man dying on a cross. [Huenemann 2009]

Respect and Dignity

Respect is the adequate regard for the feelings, wishes, rights, or traditions of others. People are becoming more and more self-centered and unsympathetic to those around them. As a result, they have little or no regard for other people's rights and feelings. Many people act without politeness, thoughtfulness, and civility. Disrespectful behavior is on the rise and people who have earned great achievements are no longer treated with the respect they deserve. Governments who treat people disrespectfully make the world a lot less peaceful. Treating people miserably is the source of unhappiness for many of them. "Life is too short to waste our time on people who don't respect, appreciate, and value us."

Dignity is the sense people have of their importance and value, and it is related to other people's respect for you. Dignity is our inherent value and worth as human beings; respect, on the other hand, is earned through one's actions. The glue that holds human relationships together is the mutual desire to be seen, heard, listened to, and treated fairly; it is also related to being recognized, understood, and to feel safe in the world. We all know the gut feeling that results from being mistreated or neglected – it is up to each one to honor other people's dignity, in the process, they strengthen their own.

Love and Empathy

Notions of love, empathy, and identification with others are fundamental in our social relationships. The psyche perceives what actually exists, but also feels or guesses what will happen in the future; this is foresight, driven by instincts. Empathy occurs between human beings, it is a natural attribute that allows coexistence. To understand somebody we need to get identified with him or her. [Adler 1992]

All of our most important emotions are bound up with some of these: erotic love, the love of children and parents, the attachment to home, the fear of death and suffering, the sympathy for others in their pain or fear – none of these things would make sense if it were not for our situation as organisms. The love of beauty, too, has its roots in our embodied life and the here and now of our joys.

Human beings find their fulfillment in mutual love and self-giving, but they get to this point via a long path of self-development, in which imitation, obedience, and self-control are necessary moments. But it is a hard thing to practice. Nevertheless, when we understand things rightly, we will be motivated to put virtue and good habits back where they belong, at the center of personal life. [Scruton 2017]

Altruism

Generosity without hope of reciprocation is the rarest and most cherished of human behaviors, subtle and difficult to define, distributed in a highly selective pattern, surrounded by ritual and circumstance, and honored by medallions and emotional orations. We sanctify true altruism to reward it and thus to make it less than true, and by that means to promote its recurrence in others. Conscious altruism is a transcendental quality that distinguishes human beings from animals.

There are two forms of cooperative behavior: "hard-core" and "soft-core" altruism. An irrational and unilaterally altruistic impulse directed at others is hard-core, serving primarily the closest relatives. Soft-core altruism, in contrast, is ultimately selfish, it expects reciprocation from society for itself or its closest relatives. [Wilson 1978]

Chapter 9: Justifications

The Homo sapiens regime on earth has so far produced little that we can be proud of. We have mastered our surroundings, increased food production, built cities, established empires and created far-flung trade networks. But did we decrease the amount of suffering in the world? Time and again, massive increases in human power did not necessarily improve the well-being of individual Sapiens and usually caused immense misery to other animals. [Harari 2014]

Humans are the outcome of blind evolutionary processes that operate without goal or purpose. Is it the task of each individual, or eventually of an authoritarian society, to define what is the purpose in life? Individually, it is an advantage because it allows people to decide their objectives. Socially, it is a disadvantage because many people would disagree with an imposed view. Individual actions are not part of some divine cosmic plan, and if planet Earth were to blow up tomorrow afternoon, the universe would probably keep going about its business, as usual, individual subjectivity would not be missed.

As far as we can tell, from a purely scientific viewpoint, human life has absolutely no meaning. Therefore, humans have plenty of alternatives to choose from, which by itself is a good thing. It would be better for humans to define their objectives early in life, even though it is difficult for many because of their lack of knowledge while young. The first thing we can discover about ourselves is that we are always striving towards a goal. The human spirit is not a single, static entity. It is a collection of moving parts. The life of the psyche requires a goal towards which all our efforts are directed. Our mental life is determined by our goals. Thinking, feeling, wishing or dreaming require an ever-present objective. [Adler 1992]

Some people may choose the wrong goals and are not able to attain them during their lifespan. However, the effort spent on the process represents a source of happiness independent of achievements. Goals should be related to the individual and society; this involves an understanding of our surroundings and the way all the participants interact. On special occasions, individuals can find activities that require little society's involvement, such as the case of artists or monks. Opportunities or lack of them always enter the life equation. Not everybody has the same opportunities in life. Knowing the goal of individuals and knowing something of the world enables people to understand the direction their life takes, and how these things function as a preparation for their goal. [Adler 1992]

Morality

Morality is concerned with our duties, but our duties all reduce, in the need, to one, which is the duty to do good – in other words, to obey those "optimistic" principles that promise the best outcome in the long run. The good person is the one who strives for the best outcome in all the moral dilemmas that he or she confronts. When asking myself what I should do, I entertain the thought of what another would think of my action when observing it with a disinterested eye. If, as I suggest, morality is rooted in the practice of accountability between self-conscious agents, this is exactly what we should expect. The impartial other sets the standard that we all must meet. [Scruton 2017]

Reasoning

One important human characteristic, which is related to the possibility of justifying results, is the capacity to reason. Without reasoning, humans cannot get along. To improve human relations, some principles of reasoning are required. Those principles establish the required balance between individuality and collectivity. The following principles seem to be accepted by those who lay down their weapons and reason toward solutions instead: [Scruton 2017]

1. Considerations that justify or impugn one person will, in identical circumstances, justify or impugn another.
2. Rights are to be respected.
3. Obligations are to be fulfilled.
4. Agreements are to be honored.
5. Disputes are to be settled by negotiation, not by force.
6. Those who do not respect the rights of others forfeit rights of their own.

Unlike Kant, Aristotle did not recognize reason as a metaphysically distinct motive; but he did think that the disposition to follow what reason commands is a real motive, one that depends on cultivating good habits and one that puts the agent in the very position that Kant sees as central to the moral life: the position of honoring obligations, despite the passions that oppose them. [Scruton 2017]

Humans differ so much on their behavior that living in a community is surrounded by conflict. Differences are sometimes influenced by family, other times by culture, and other times by personality. Those differences determine how prone we are to comply with the principles of reasoning. Those principles have no frontier, therefore, any society can use them for purposes of educating their citizens.

The peculiar force of morality and the sense of duty set us outside and against the order of nature. We are law-governed creatures, and even when we defy the law, we act on the assumption that we are subject to nonnegotiable demands – reasons that have the power to silence countervailing considerations, however closely they represent our empirical interests. [Scruton 2017]

We do not need to suppose a "causality of reason" to make sense of the soldier's predicament. We need only recognize that the soldier like every person, has a sense of obligation – a sense of promises given and received, of relations to others that depend on his loyalty, of responsibilities undertaken, all of which are stored in his thinking in a place apart. These things are stored in the I, as commitments "to be honored," and have a distinct status in defining the soldier's sense of who he is. To dishonor them is possible; but the price of doing so is guilt, remorse, and adverse judgment of the self by the self, such as blighted the life of Conrad's Lord Jim. [Scruton 2017]

People come to depend on each other in many ways. The most significant environments requiring reasoning are family relations, warfare, duties of charity, and justice toward strangers. These environments require negotiated terms, however, not all parties have the same understanding of what good reasoning is. Morality exists in part because it enables us to live on negotiated terms with others. We can do this because we act for reasons and respond to reasons too. When we incur the displeasure of those around us, we attempt to justify our actions, and it is part of our accountability that we should reach for principles that others too can accept and which are perforce impartial, universal, and law-like. [Scruton 2017]

When faced with a policy issue, a normal thought process should go something like this: [Steele 2017]
- Define the problem you are trying to solve.
- Identify the causes of the problem.
- Develop policy options to resolve the causes.
- Select the best policy option.

- Decide on an implementation and communication plan.
- Implement and communicate.

Negotiation

Negotiation is a popular term these days but most people have difficulties accepting other's opinions and reaching consensus. Frequently people prefer confrontation and isolation instead of negotiation. Humans need to follow some principles to live in a society and they should be known by everybody. However, most people are aware of those recommendations but they do not follow them.

Negotiation is an art, it requires intelligence, empathy, justice, and resolution. Negotiation requires an open mind ready to produce acceptable alternatives. Negotiation also needs creativity, obtuse minds are the worst participants in negotiation. Good negotiation requires that you first be creative about how to serve each side's interests, and only then get down to the business of choosing options. [Steele 2017]

Negotiation requires morality. The fundamental intuition is that morality exists in part because it enables us to live on negotiated terms with others. We can do this because we act for reasons and respond to reasons too. When we incur the displeasure of those around us, we attempt to justify our actions, and it is part of our accountability that we should reach for principles that others too can accept and which are perforce impartial, universal, and lawlike. [Scruton 2017]

Politicians are frequently involved in a negotiation because they are running a business, and the business they're in is called re-election. You need to think of your interaction with politicians as a business negotiation. People are negotiating the scarce allocation of public resources and the allocation of the politician's interest and energy. [Steele 2017]

'The Getting to Yes' method is built on four basic ideas: [Steele 2017]
- Separate the people from the problem;
- Focus on interests, not positions;
- Invent options for mutual gain;
- Insist on using objective criteria.

Good negotiation requires that people understand the other side's position. The ability to see the situation as the other side sees it is part of the solution. Those that only see their side are going to have a hard time during a negotiation. Good negotiation requires that people focus on the needs, desires, concerns, and fears of each side. These are their interests, and they are not the same as the other side's position, which is how they want their interests to be served. Positions come and go; interests are steady or at least evolve very slowly. Good negotiations focus on interests. [Steele 2017]

Part III: Human Influence

Human behavior is determined by many human characteristics that affect individuals in multiple degrees. Humans have weaknesses that define their behavior. It is important to be familiarized with human weaknesses because political systems, in many cases, benefit from them. Human weaknesses are used for the good and the bad in political systems. Socialism is a system that benefits from human weaknesses to stay in power and not to benefit the population.

Are people happier? Did the wealth humankind accumulated over the last five centuries translate into new-found contentment? Probably not, humans are quite difficult to please. There is always going to be some happy and some unhappy. The evaluation must be done on the infrastructure built around the productive and unproductive organizations that create opportunities for a better life. Socialism fails at the individual and society levels because they don't organize the activities for the benefit of the population.

Humans have clear limitations in paying attention, wrong things happen in front of their eyes and they are incapable of responding with the best approach. Socialists benefit of human weaknesses to stay in power without convincing or demonstrating any tendency to prosperity.

People depend on emotions, it is a natural way of manifesting behavior. Socialists play with the emotional side of humans and exploit such weaknesses on their benefit or to benefit their elite.

Most people are superstitious and it does not mean they believe in supernatural forces. Socialists tend to attach supernatural forces to their leaders to exploit the natural inclination of people toward miraculous coincidences.

Responsibility is the feeling of holding each other accountable for what they do and it includes ourselves. Responsibility is a natural human trait that should be extended to the political system, if the government does not perform, it should renounce and let capable citizens take charge.

How do we separate fantasy from reality? People always create their fictive vision of their life and when suffering tends to accept the conditions imposed by the regime. Socialists benefit of this characteristic to keep people outside of the important decisions of the society.

Humans are primarily egocentrics and they have no choice. Socialists benefit from this weakness by pleasing survival instincts such as hunger or health; socialists control the distribution of food and medicines to guarantee their support to stay eternally in power.

Judgment, both conscious and unconscious, is a fundamental part of the human experience. Socialists must understand that they are going to be judged on results not on words or paper. If socialism does not perform, it must take his baggage and abandon power, that would be a contribution to the universe.

Unusual reactions are a characteristic of humans. Human responses use to be unexpected, there is much human imagination involved. Socialism should be more imaginative and understand its failure. There is no theoretical or practical demonstration of its effectiveness.

Chapter 10: Human Happiness

There are many interpretations of happiness, starting at the individual level up to the whole population. Humans are the main recipients of happiness, they are the ones looking for explanations. The consequences of people's actions stretch infinitely outward in both space and time. The best of intentions can lead to the worst of results. And values are many and in tension with each other. What place should people accord to beauty, grace, and dignity – or do these all creep into their deliberations as parts of human happiness? ... what happiness consists of, by what scale it should be measured, or what human beings gain from their aesthetic and spiritual values? [Scruton 2017]

Philosophers, priests, and poets have brooded over the nature of happiness for millennia, and many have concluded that social, ethical and spiritual factors have as great an impact on our happiness as material conditions. Happiness is a sense of well-being, joy, or contentment. When people are enjoying life, feel successful, or safe, or lucky, they feel happy. Whenever doing something causes happiness, people usually want to do more of it. No one has ever complained about feeling too much happiness.

In recent decades, psychologists and biologists have taken up the challenge of studying scientifically what makes people happy. Is it money, family, genetics or perhaps virtue? The first step is to define what is to be measured. The generally accepted definition of happiness is 'subjective well-being'. Happiness, according to this view, is something people feel inside, a sense of either immediate pleasure or long-term contentment with the way their life is going. [Harari 2014]

One interesting conclusion of published psychological research is that money does indeed bring happiness. But only up to a point, and beyond that, it has little significance. Another interesting finding is that illness decreases happiness in the short term, but is a source of long-term distress only if a person's condition is constantly deteriorating or if the disease involves ongoing and debilitating pain.

Family and community seem to have more impact on people's happiness than money and health. People with strong families who live in tight-knit and supportive communities are significantly happier than people whose families are dysfunctional and who have never found (or never sought) a community to be part of. Marriage is particularly important. But the most important finding of all is that happiness does not depend on objective conditions of either wealth, health or even community. Rather, it depends on the correlation between objective conditions and subjective expectations. [Harari 2014]

But are people happier? Did the wealth humankind accumulated over the last five centuries translate into new-found contentment? Did the discovery of inexhaustible energy resources open before us inexhaustible stores of bliss? Going further back, have the seventy or so turbulent millennia since the Cognitive Revolution made the world a better place to live? Was the late Neil Armstrong, whose footprint remains intact on the windless moon, happier than the nameless hunter-gatherer who 30,000 years ago left her handprint on a wall in the Chauvet Cave? If not, what was the point of developing agriculture, cities, writing, coinage, empires, science and industry? [Harari 2014]

Yet these are the most important questions one can ask of history. Most current ideologies and political programs are based on rather flimsy ideas concerning the real source of human happiness. Nationalists believe that political self-determination is essential for their happiness. Communists postulate that everyone would be blissful under the dictatorship of the proletariat. Capitalists maintain that only the free market can ensure the greatest happiness of the greatest number, by creating economic growth and material abundance and by teaching people to be self-reliant and enterprising. [Harari 2014]

<u>Human Expectations</u>

The crucial importance of human expectations has far-reaching implications for understanding the history of happiness. If happiness depended only on objective conditions such as wealth, health and social relations, it would have been relatively easy to investigate its history. The finding that it depends on subjective expectations makes the task of historians far harder. We moderns have an arsenal of tranquilizers and painkillers at our disposal, but our expectations of ease and pleasure, and our intolerance of inconvenience and discomfort have increased to such an extent that we may well suffer from pain more than our ancestors ever did. [Harari 2014]

If happiness is determined by expectations, then two pillars of our society – mass media and the advertising industry – may unwittingly be depleting the globe's reservoirs of contentment. So maybe Third World discontent is fomented not merely by poverty, disease, corruption, and political oppression but also by mere exposure to First World standards. [Harari 2014]

When we try to guess or imagine how happy other people are now, or how happy people in the past were, we inevitably imagine ourselves in their shoes. But that won't work because it pastes our expectations on to the material conditions of others. The life of medieval peasants compared with modern affluent societies was different. How medieval peasants felt at the time was based on the characteristics of their life, their entourage and the environment. They had specific needs and they were happy according to their possibilities. Modern societies live on other conditions, therefore, their expectations are completely different.

Subjective and Objective Happiness

Some views share the assumption that happiness is some sort of subjective feeling (of either pleasure or meaning), and that to judge people's happiness, all we need to do is ask them how they feel. To many of us, that seems logical because the dominant religion of our age is liberalism. Liberalism sanctifies the subjective feelings of individuals. 'Be true to yourself', 'Listen to yourself', 'Follow your heart'. Jean-Jacques Rousseau stated this view most classically: 'What I feel to be good – is good. What I feel to be bad – is bad.'

Religions and ideologies throughout history stated that there are objective yardsticks for goodness and beauty, and for how things ought to be. They were suspicious of the feelings and preferences of the ordinary person. At the entrance of the temple of Apollo at Delphi, pilgrims were greeted by the inscription: 'Know thyself!' The implication was that the average person is ignorant of his true self, and is therefore likely to be ignorant of true happiness.

Biological Happiness

Biologists hold that our mental and emotional world is governed by biochemical mechanisms shaped by millions of years of evolution. Like all other mental states, our subjective well-being is not determined by external parameters such as salary, social relations or political rights. Rather, it is determined by a complex system of nerves, neurons, synapses and various biochemical substances such as serotonin, dopamine, and oxytocin. [Harari 2014]

People are happy by winning the lottery, buying a house, buying a car, getting a promotion or even finding true love. However, the real sensation is not external, it happens into their bodies. People are made happy by one thing and one thing only – pleasant sensations in their bodies. A person who just won the lottery or found a new love and jumps from joy is not reacting to the money or the lover. She is reacting to various hormones coursing through her bloodstream, and to the storm of electric signals ashing between different parts of her brain. [Harari 2014]

Unfortunately, people are programmed to keep happiness levels relatively constant. There's no natural selection for happiness as such – a happy hermit's genetic line will go extinct as the genes of a pair of anxious parents get carried on to the next generation. Happiness and misery play a role in evolution only to the extent that they encourage or discourage survival and reproduction. Perhaps it's not surprising, then, that evolution has shaped us to be neither too miserable nor too happy. It enables us to enjoy a momentary rush of pleasant sensations, but these never last forever. Sooner or later they subside and give place to unpleasant sensations. [Harari 2014]

History turns out to be of minor importance since most historical events have had no impact on our biochemistry. Take, for example, the French Revolution. The revolutionaries were busy: they executed the king, gave lands to the peasants, declared the rights of man, abolished noble privileges and waged war against the whole of Europe. Yet none of that changed French biochemistry. Consequently, despite all the political, social, ideological and economic upheavals brought about by the revolution, its impact on French happiness was small. Those who won cheerful biochemistry in the genetic lottery were just as happy before the revolution as after. Those with gloomy biochemistry complained about Robespierre and Napoleon with the same bitterness with which they earlier complained about Louis XVI and Marie Antoinette. [Harari 2014]

The keys to happiness are in the hands of our biochemical system. In Aldous Huxley's dystopian novel Brave New World, published in 1932 at the height of the Great Depression, happiness is the supreme value and psychiatric drugs replace the police and the ballot as the foundation of politics. Each day, each person takes a dose of 'soma', a synthetic drug that makes people happy without harming their productivity and efficiency. The World State that governs the entire globe is never threatened by wars, revolutions, strikes or demonstrations because all people are supremely content with their current conditions, whatever they may be.

Huxley's disconcerting world is based on the biological assumption that happiness equals pleasure. To be happy is no more and no less than experiencing pleasant bodily sensations. Since our biochemistry limits the volume and duration of these sensations, the only way to make people experience a high level of happiness over an extended period is to manipulate their biochemical system.

Meaningfulness

Although people in all cultures and eras have felt the same type of pleasures and pains, the meaning they have ascribed to their experiences has probably varied widely. If so, the history of happiness might have been far more turbulent than biologists imagine. Medieval people believed the promise of everlasting bliss in the afterlife, they viewed their lives as far more meaningful and worthwhile than modern secular people, who in the long term can expect nothing but complete and meaningless oblivion. Asked 'Are you satisfied with your life as a whole?' people in the Middle Ages might have scored quite high in a subjective well-being questionnaire. So our medieval ancestors were happy because they found meaning to life in collective delusions about the afterlife? Yes.

Hence any meaning that people ascribe to their lives is just a delusion. The otherworldly meanings medieval people found in their lives were no more deluded than the modern humanist, nationalist and capitalist meanings modern people find. The scientist who says her life is meaningful because she increases the store of human knowledge, the soldier who declares that his life is meaningful because he fights to defend his homeland, and the entrepreneur who finds meaning in building a new company is no less delusional than their medieval counterparts who found meaning in reading scriptures, going on a crusade or building a new cathedral.

In a famous study, Daniel Kahneman, winner of the Nobel Prize in economics, asked people to recount a typical workday, going through it episode by episode and evaluating how much they enjoyed or disliked each moment. He discovered what seems to be a paradox in most people's view of their lives. Take the work involved in raising a child. Kahneman found that when counting moments of joy and moments of drudgery, bringing up a child turns out to be a rather unpleasant affair. It consists largely of changing nappies, washing dishes and dealing with temper tantrums, which nobody likes to do. Yet most parents declare that their children are their chief source of happiness. Does it mean that people don't know what's good for them?

That's one option. Another is that the findings demonstrate that happiness is not the surplus of pleasant over unpleasant moments. Rather, happiness consists in seeing one's life in its entirety as meaningful and worthwhile. There is an important cognitive and ethical component to happiness. Our values make all the difference to whether we see ourselves as 'miserable slaves to a baby dictator' or as 'lovingly nurturing a new life'. As Nietzsche put it, if you have a why to live, you can bear almost any how. A meaningful life can be extremely satisfying even amid hardship, whereas a meaningless life is a terrible ordeal no matter how comfortable it is.

Buddhism and Happiness

Religions and philosophies have consequently taken a very different approach to happiness than liberalism does. The Buddhist position is particularly interesting. For Buddhism, the question of happiness is more important than perhaps any other human creed. For 2,500 years, Buddhists have systematically studied the essence and causes of happiness, which is why there is a growing interest among the scientific community both in their philosophy and their meditation practices.

Buddhism shares the basic insight of the biological approach to happiness, namely that happiness results from processes occurring within one's body, and not from events in the outside world. However, starting with the same insight, Buddhism reaches very different conclusions. According to Buddhism, most people identify happiness with pleasant feelings, while identifying suffering with unpleasant feelings. People consequently ascribe immense importance to what they feel, craving to experience more and more pleasures while avoiding pain.

The problem, according to Buddhism, is that our feelings are no more than fleeting vibrations, changing every moment, like the ocean waves. If five minutes ago I felt joyful and purposeful, now these feelings are gone, and I might well feel sad and dejected. So if I want to experience pleasant feelings, I have to constantly chase them, while driving away from the unpleasant feelings. Even if I succeed, I immediately have to start all over again, without ever getting any lasting reward for my troubles.

The real root of suffering is this never-ending and pointless pursuit of ephemeral feelings, which causes us to be in a constant state of tension, restlessness, and dissatisfaction. Due to this pursuit, the mind is never satisfied. Even when experiencing pleasure, it is not content, because it fears this feeling might soon disappear and craves that this feeling should stay and intensify. People are liberated from suffering not when they experience this or that fleeting pleasure, but rather when they understand the impermanent nature of all their feelings and stop craving them. This is the aim of Buddhist meditation practices.

To sum up, subjective well-being questionnaires identify our well-being with our subjective feelings and identify the pursuit of happiness with the pursuit of particular emotional states. In contrast, for many traditional philosophies and religions, such as Buddhism, the key to happiness is to know the truth about yourself – to understand who, or what, you are. Most people wrongly identify themselves with their feelings, thoughts, likes, and dislikes. When they feel anger, they think, 'I am angry. This is my anger.' They consequently spend their life avoiding some kinds of feelings and pursuing others. They never realize that they are not their feelings and that the relentless pursuit of particular feelings just traps them in misery.

If this is so, then our entire understanding of the history of happiness might be misguided. Maybe it isn't so important whether people's expectations are fulfilled and whether they enjoy pleasant feelings. The main question is whether people know the truth about themselves. What evidence do we have that people today understand this truth any better than ancient foragers or medieval peasants?

Chapter 11: Attention and Memory

Humans have clear limitations in paying attention, either noticing someone or identifying something interesting. Attention involves the act or will of carefully thinking about, listening to, or watching someone or something. Attention requires concentration, the act of keeping one's mind focused on something which implies some effort. Attention is also the awareness of the here and now in a focal and perceptive way; sometimes paying attention to some phenomenon and excluding other stimuli.

Human Limitations (Attention)
People have natural limitations paying attention to daily activities of their life. People are aware only of a small amount of the total information their eyes take in and even less is processed by their conscious mind and remembered. People are not capable of seeing everything going on before their eyes and much less taking in all the information like a camera. Focusing their attention on one thing, everything else blurs into the periphery. [McRaney 2011]

People pay attention only to certain things to create their moment-to-moment perception of reality. Everything else is lost or blurred. It happens with the information coming through their eyeballs. They don't notice it as much when they do it visually. The world outside people's heads and the world inside are not identical. The information flowing into consciousness from people's senses is not only limited by their attention but also edited before it arrives. Once there, it mixes like paint with all the other thoughts and perceptions swirling inside people's brains.

The way people feel, the culture they grew up in, the task at hand, the chaos of technology and society – it all creates a granular, busy visual world. Only a slice of it arrives in their mind. Despite this, the great circus of human activity and invention goes on. People choose what to see more than they realize, and then they form beliefs without taking into account their selective vision.

Missing information in plain sight is called inattentional blindness. People see only a small portion of their environment at any moment. Inattentional blindness happens often but people don't believe it happens. Instead, people believe they see the whole world in front of them.

People believe with confidence their eyes capture everything before them and their memories are recorded versions of those captured images.

The truth, though, is people see only a small portion of their environment at any one moment. Their attention is like a spotlight, and only the illuminated portions of the world appear in their perception.

<u>Influencing memory</u> (The Misinformation Effect)

It is a well-known phenomenon to lose memories after some time has passed. When we learn a new subject, we start losing the memory of the information after a few months, after a year we may forget everything. And memories are constructed anew each time from whatever information is currently available, which makes them highly permeable to influences from the present. It isn't true that memories are played back like recordings. [McRaney 2011]

Every once in awhile someone tells a story that conflicts with our recollection. Not only is our memory easily altered by the influence of others, but we also smooth over the incongruences, rearrange timelines, and invent scenarios, but rarely notice we're doing this until we see ourselves in a video, or hear another person's version of the events.

We tend to see our memories as a continuous, consistent movie, yet if we think of the last film we saw, how much of it can we recall? Could we sit back, close our eyes, and recall in perfect detail every scene, every line of dialog? Of course not, so why do we assume we can do the same for the movie of our life?

Memory is imperfect, but also constantly changing. Not only do we filter our past through our present, but our memory is easily infected by social contagion. We incorporate the memories of others into our heads all the time.

Studies suggest our memory is permeable, malleable, and evolving. It isn't fixed and permanent, but more like a dream that pulls in information about what we are thinking about during the day and adds new details to the narrative. If we suppose it could have happened, we are far less likely to question ourselves as to whether it did.

<u>Being Influenced</u> (Priming)

Priming is a characteristic involving the influence of the subconscious. People are unaware of the constant nudging received from ideas formed in their unconscious minds. It isn't true that people know when they are being influenced and how it is affecting their behavior. People think they know how the world works, but they don't. People create narratives, little stories to explain away why they acted in some manner. [McRaney 2011]

The subjective experience is split into consciousness and subconsciousness all the time. People are doing it right now – breathing, blinking, swallowing, maintaining their posture, and holding their mouth closed while they read. People could pull those systems into conscious control or leave them to the autonomic nervous system. People could sing along with their friends while the other parts of their mind handle the mundane stuff. People accept their unconscious mind as just another weird component of the human experience, but they tend to see it as a separate thing – a primal self underneath consciousness that doesn't have the combination of the safe.

Priming happens when a stimulus in the past affects the way people behave and think or the way they perceive another stimulus later on. Every perception, no matter if consciously noticed, sets off a chain of related ideas in people's neural networks. Pencils make you think of pens. Blackboards make you think of classrooms. It happens to people all the time, and though they are unaware, it changes the way they behave. The subconscious mind influences the rest of people's thinking and behavior and it is easily influenced by priming.

Priming works best when people are on autopilot when they aren't trying to consciously introspect before choosing how to behave. When people are unsure how best to proceed, suggestions bubble up from the deep that are highly tainted by subconscious primes. Besides, our brain hates ambiguity and is willing to take shortcuts to remove it from any situation.

We can prime potential employers with what we wear to a job interview. People can prime the emotions of their guests with how they set the mood when hosting a party. Once people know priming is a fact of life, they start to understand the power and resilience of rituals and rites of passage, norms, and ideologies. Systems designed to prime persist because they work. Starting tomorrow, maybe with just a smile and a thank-you, people can affect the way others feel – hopefully for the best.

Chapter 12: Emotions

The world is full of interactions between humans, they respond to others with emotions that lie beyond the repertory of other animals: indignation, resentment, envy, admiration, commitment, and praise – all of which involve the thought of others as accountable subjects, with rights and duties and a self-conscious vision of their future and their past. Only responsible beings can feel these emotions, and in feeling them, they situate themselves in some way outside the natural order, standing back from it in judgment. [Scruton 2017]

Emotions such as resentment, guilt, gratitude, and anger are not human versions of responses that we might observe in other animals but ways in which the demand for accountability, which arises spontaneously between creatures who can know themselves as "I," translates into the language of feelings. [Scruton 2017]

<u>Anger</u>

Humans are prone to strong feelings of annoyance, displeasure, and hostility. When people think that someone has behaved in an unfair, cruel, or unacceptable way, they may shout with anger and frustration. Anger is an intense emotional state, it involves a strong, uncomfortable and hostile response to a provocation, hurt, or threat.

<u>Fear</u>

Humans feel sometimes an unpleasant, often strong emotion caused by anticipation or awareness of danger. Fear involves some other emotions such as anxiety, dread or fearfulness that in some situations can develop into terror.

<u>Human's Dark Side</u>

The human brain is apt to good and bad things. Human beings are traditionally dark on their appreciation of things. Too much idleness can create a dangerous environment attempting to people's health. To maintain sanity people must work every day, preferably in productive activities that contribute to society. Several wrongful emotions can be attached to humans. There is a close relationship between greed and envy, as well as a connection with ambition and vanity. All these may be present at the same time. [Adler 1992]

We have to distinguish people who are evil from those who are merely bad. Bad people are like you or me, only worse. They belong to the community, even if they behave badly toward it. We can reason with them, improve them, come to terms with them, and, in the end, accept them. They are made, like us, from "the crooked timber of humanity." Evil people are not like that since they do not belong in the community, even if residing within its territory. Their bad behavior may be too secret and subversive to be noticeable, and any dialogue with them will be, on their part, a pretense. There is in them, no scope for improvement, no path to acceptance, and even if we think of them as human, their faults are not of the normal, remedial human variety but have another and more metaphysical origin. They are, in some sense, the negation of humanity, wholly and unnaturally at ease with the things that they seek to destroy. [Scruton 2017]

Evil people try to destroy others' mindfulness. The characterization of evil is summarized in the famous line that Goethe gives to Mephistopheles: "Ich bin der Geist, der stetsverneint" [I am the spirit that forever negates]. Whereas the bad person is guided by self-interest, to the point of ignoring or overriding the others who stand in his or her path, the evil person is profoundly interested in others, has almost selfless designs on them. The aim is not to use them, as Faust uses Gretchen, but to rob them of themselves. Mephistopheles hopes to steal and destroy Faust's soul and, en route to that end, to destroy the soul of Gretchen. Evil people are not necessarily threats to your body, but they are threats to your self.[Scruton 2017]

Definitively, bad people abound. Everybody has had experiences with bad people, for example, people not honoring their compromises, people making benefits from others, people stealing from others, people mortifying others, and so on. However, evil people are much more dangerous, they are bad and capable of endangering everybody. They may look friendly but you can notice their twisted feelings. Some are willing to give advice, and unless you are naïve, you notice their malignant purposes. They try to get the confidence to influence negatively your life, it is you that has to be smart and avoid their company. Sometimes, this evil behavior is driven by envy.

Non-violent Strategies

There are positive strategies to avoid violence, for example, "If our first response to injury is not violence but blame, the other is allowed to make amends. Violence is forestalled or postponed, and a process can then begin – the process that is well described in the Roman Catholic theology of repentance – whereby guilty parties are first marginalized and then, through atonement and contrition, reincluded, their fault duly forgiven. It is obvious that communities that can resolve their conflicts in this way have a competitive advantage over those whose only response to injury is violence." [Scruton 2017]

To avoid deaths during the war, some non-violent strategies are preferred, "The habit of capitulation rather than fighting to the end over territory and mates likewise has a life-preserving and therefore general preserving function." Having the opportunity to express your thoughts is also a source of promoting peace, "When you rightly accuse me of injuring you, I may look for excuses, and there is an elaborate dialogue here through which we express our intuitions concerning the avoidable and the unavoidable." [Scruton 2017]

Expressing guilt is another strategy to prevent additional violence, "Guilt feelings may be more or less strong, some people are experts at entertaining them, and they prompt the great yearning which engages with our most urgent loves and fears in this world: the yearning for redemption, for the blessing that relieves us of our guilt. Glimpses of this blessing are afforded by such liminal experiences as falling in love, recovering from illness, becoming a parent, and encountering in awe the sublime works of nature." [Scruton 2017]

The path of reconciliation is preferable to the eternal pursuit of conflict. Good and evil, sacred and profane, redemption, purity, and sacrifice all then make sense to us, and we are along a path of reconciliation, both to the people around us and to our destiny as dying things. Even for those who do not consider the dogmas of religion to be true, the religious posture, and the rituals that express it provides another kind of support to the moral life. Religion, on this understanding, is a dedication of one's being." [Scruton 2017]

<u>Vanity</u>

Vanity is excessive pride in one's appearance, qualities, abilities, achievements, and it is also referred to as the character or quality of being vain. It is a human nature trait that cannot be eliminated. Vanity should be reduced to help soften eccentric behavior and return people to collaborative behavior. Logic and reasoning used to change up people's minds and contribute towards a better society. Vanity and cooperation are the antagonist. In an age like ours, which demands so much cooperation, there is no longer place for the striving of personal vanity. [Adler 1992]

Envy

Envy is a feeling of discontent or covetousness about other's advantages, successes, possessions, etc. It is universally disliked by human beings. Very few people, however, do not feel envy sometimes. None is entirely free from it. When life runs smoothly this may not often be evident. But when people are in pain, or feel oppressed, or lack money, food, clothes or warmth, when their hope for the future is darkened and they see no way out of their unfortunate situation, then envy appears. [Adler 1992]

Socialism is based on envy. People lacking basic facilities are prone to envy, the state in Venezuela has been in charge of making people poorer year after year. To reduce envy, people must be occupied doing useful things, idleness creates dangerous vices that jeopardize a healthy society. Socialism offers a life without work, where people pass their time doing nothing.

Emotions guide decisions (The Affect Heuristic)

The affect heuristic stands out the importance of emotions. People depend on emotions to tell if something is good or bad, greatly overestimate rewards and tend to stick on their first impressions. It isn't true that people calculate what is risky or rewarding and always choose to maximize gains while minimizing losses. [McRaney 2011]

The tendency to make poor decisions and ignore odds in favor of our gut feelings is called the affect heuristic. It is always getting between us and our best interests, and it starts when we make a snap judgment about something new.

The first time we meet someone, billions of micro thoughts ricochet through the chemical and electrical conduits in our cranium. We begin making judgments about the person's character before we realize it. We may notice a handshake that is strong and vigorous, that the person's posture is forward and sturdy, that his or her smile is perfect and warm. We take all these features and multiply them by how the person is dressed, divide by the way the person smells, and factor age into a huge equation that forms the first impression in our unconscious. This person is good. Let's get to know this person.

The affect heuristic is one way we rapidly conclude new information. We use it to drop data into two broad categories – good and bad – and then we choose to avoid or seek out what we have judged. The affect heuristic is the Holy Grail of cognitive biases in advertising and politics. When we can associate our product or candidate with positive things or our competitors and opponents with negative things, we win. If we build up enough associations, our product can become eponymous with the category it occupies. Facial tissues become Kleenex. Pain medicine becomes Aspirin. Bandages become BandAids.

There is debate among psychologists on just how powerful and trustworthy snap decisions are, but there is no doubt they play a large role in who we are and how we interpret our senses. When first impressions linger and influence how we feel about second, third, and fourth impressions, we are being befuddled by the affect heuristic.

The affect heuristic, therefore, is often a good thing. We need it to see danger and pick a place to eat after a concert. The problems arise when we must evaluate large numbers or percentages when we must see connections and abstractions. This is why politicians who bring out charts and graphs tend to fail, and those who use anecdotes tend to win. Stories make sense on an emotional level, so anything that conjures fear, empathy, or pride will trump confusing statistics.

<u>Emotion is Tricky</u> (Introspection)

Introspection is a behavior related to the difficulty to explain people's decisions. The origin of certain emotional states is unavailable to people, and when pressed to explain them, they will just make something up. It isn't true that people know why they like the things they like and feel the way they feel. [McRaney 2011]

When faced with a decision in which people are forced to think about their rationale, they start to turn the volume in their emotional brain down and the volume in their logical brain up. People start creating a mental list of pros and cons that would never have been conjured up if they had gone with their gut.

Ruminations about our depression tend to make us more depressed, but distraction leads to an improved mood. Sometimes, introspection is simply counterproductive. Research into introspection calls into question the entire industry of critical analysis of art – video games, music, film, poetry, literature – all of it. It also makes things like focus groups and market analysis seem less about the intrinsic quality of the things being judged and more about what the people doing the judging find to be plausible explanations of their feelings.

When asking people why they do or don't like things, they must translate from a deep, emotional, primal part of their psyche into the language of the higher, logical, rational world of words and sentences and paragraphs.

Believing people understand their motivations and desires, their likes and dislikes is called the introspection illusion. People believe they know themselves and why they are the way they are. People believe this knowledge tells them how they will act in all future situations. Research shows otherwise. Time after time, experiments show introspection is not the act of tapping into their innermost mental constructs but is instead a fabrication. People look at what they did, or how they felt, and they make up some sort of explanation that they can reasonably believe. If they have to tell others, they make up an explanation they can believe too.

Confirming what you Believe (Confirmation Bias)

Confirmation bias reflects the tendency of people to define their decisions on concepts they already know. People's opinion is the result of years of paying attention to information that confirmed what they believed while ignoring information that challenged their preconceived notions. It isn't true that people's opinions are the result of years of rational, objective analysis. [McRaney 2011]

If you are thinking about buying a particular make of a new car, you suddenly see people driving that car all over the roads. If you just ended a longtime relationship, every song you hear seems to be written about love. If you are having a baby, you start to see babies everywhere. Confirmation bias is seeing the world through a filter.

Be careful. People like to be told what they already know. Remember that. They get uncomfortable when you tell them new things. New things . . . well, new things aren't what they expect. They like to know that, say, a snake will bite a man. That is what snakes do. They don't want to know that man bites a snake, because the world is not supposed to happen like that. In short, what people think they want is news, but what they crave is olds . . . Not news but olds, telling people that what they think they already know is true.

Journalists looking to tell a certain story must avoid the tendency to ignore evidence to the contrary; scientists looking to prove a hypothesis must avoid designing experiments with little wiggle room for alternate outcomes. Without confirmation bias, conspiracy theories would fall apart. Did we put a man on the moon? If you are looking for proof we didn't, you can find it.

People buy books for confirmation. They want to be right about how they see the world, so they seek out information that confirms their beliefs and avoid contradictory evidence and opinions.

Misleading Expectations (Expectations)

Expectations can be altered to fool experts, consumers, and the population. It isn't true that experts are impervious to deception. [McRaney 2011]

The expectation is a nasty beast. Expectation, as it turns out, is just as important as raw sensation. The buildup to experience can completely change how we interpret the information. Wine experts get mislead when the environment is manipulated; their objectivity and powers of taste get mislead.

True objectivity is pretty much considered to be impossible (psychology). Memories, emotions, conditioning taint every new experience. Some expectations come from within and some come from without. Expensive wine builds the expectation that it tastes better. Testing TV sets: the expectation of seeing a better-quality image led people to believe they had. Pepsi and coke marketing campaigns help to sell the product.

You look for clues from the environment whenever you find things you like. Vodka has no taste, therefore, advertisement is needed. Taste is subjective, you are not so smart when choosing one product over another. All things being equal – packaging and advertisement or conformity with your friends and family. The presentation is everything. Presentation, price, good marketing, great service – it all leads to an expectation of quality.

The experience at the end of all this is less important, as long as it is not total crap. Your experience will match up with your expectations. Your expectations are the horse, and your experience is the cart. You get this backward all the time because you are not so smart.

Mislead by Appearances (The Anchoring Effect)

The anchoring effect is a characteristic that influences people's behavior. People's first perception lingers in their minds, affecting later perceptions and decisions. It isn't true that people rationally analyze all factors before making a choice or determining value. They don't tend to use some situations as their reference to make comparisons. Bad situations shouldn't be considered as common, and worst of all, people shouldn't get used to them. People should facilitate change because they shouldn't get used to bad situations. [McRaney 2011]

People depend on anchoring every day to predict the outcome of events, to estimate how much time something will take or how much money something will cost. When choosing between options, or estimating a value, people need footing to stand on.

This is why in a negotiation, people should make their initial request far too high. People have to start somewhere and the initial decision or calculation greatly influences all the choices that follow, cascading out, each tethered to the anchors set before.

Many choices being done every day are reruns of past decisions; as if traveling channels dug into a dirt road by a wagon train of selections, people follow the path created by their former self.

External anchors, like prices before a sale or ridiculous requests, are obvious and can be avoided. Internal, self-generated anchors are not so easy to bypass. People communicate with the same friends every day, eat the same type of breakfast, and follow the same sex routine with their partners. These choices, so predictable – ask what drives them. Are old anchors controlling peoples' current decisions?

Anchoring can be used to manipulate people to do good. For example, when people are asked to volunteer in activities over long periods, most people don't accept the task, however, if the activities are over a short period, the percentage of people accepting the task increases.

Recognizing Weaknesses (Hindsight Bias)

The hindsight effect is a behavior where people don't accept their ignorance. People often look back on the things they have just learned and assume they knew them or believed them all along. It isn't true that after people learn something new, they remember how they were once ignorant or wrong. [McRaney 2011]

People tend to edit their memories so they don't seem like such a dimwit when things happen a way they couldn't have predicted. When people learn things they wish they had known all along, they go ahead and assume they did know them. People believe anecdote and individual sensational news stories are more representatives of the big picture than they are.

The availability heuristic shows you make decisions and think thoughts based on the information you have at hand while ignoring all the other information out there. Thinking thoughts and making decisions based on what you know now, not what you used to know. On an argument, the other person does think it was never wrong, and so do you.

People's Inconsistency (Consistency Bias)

Consistency bias is a response people show to maintain continuity. Unless people consciously keep tabs on their progress, they assume the way they feel now is the way they have always felt. It isn't true that people know how their opinions have changed over time. [McRaney 2011]

People naturally change over time, but the failure to admit it demonstrates consistency bias. People need to feel they can predict their behavior, so they rewrite their history to seem dependable.

If people are primed to be honest, they act as if they are. People want to be consistent, they don't want to be hypocrites. Saying one thing and doing another, means the feeling of being hypocrite must be dealt with before proceeding with life.

Whatever people feel they were when young, likely it is different from what they are now. When people are young, they are more open to change their opinions. After gaining enough life experience, people begin to settle into a view of the world and establish their moral outlook.

Chapter 13: Credulity

Human beings are naturally superstitious, some examples are believing in God or spirits, or believing in the afterlife. Luckily, many people believe in causality, that things happen without any particular intervention of a fictive deity. Superstition is an excessively credulous belief in and reverence for supernatural causes leading to certain consequences of an action or event, or a practice based on such an event. Most of us are superstitious and it does not mean we believe in supernatural forces; most superstitions are popular beliefs people repeat over and over; Friday the thirteenth, crossing a black cat, passing under a ladder, and so on. Let us take faith, we use to have faith in the future, on feeling happiness, on having health, and so on, independently of religion. We also tend to believe things that happen are the consequence of our mistakes, let us take marriage, we use to think that if we had listened to the advice of our parents we had made a better choice for a spouse.

Ancient Foragers' Superstition

We have only the haziest notions about the religions of ancient foragers. We assume that they were animists, but that's not very informative. We don't know which spirits they prayed to, which festivals they celebrated, or which taboos they observed. Animism (from 'anima,' 'soul' or 'spirit' in Latin) is the belief that almost every place, every animal, every plant and every natural phenomenon has awareness and feelings, and can communicate directly with humans. [Harari 2014]

Religion

Today's religion is often considered a source of discrimination, disagreement, and disunion. Yet, religion has been the third great unifier of humankind, alongside with money and empires. Since all social orders and hierarchies are imagined, they are all fragile, and the larger the society, the more fragile they are. The crucial historical role of religion has been to give superhuman legitimacy to these fragile structures. Religions assert that our laws are not the result of human caprice, but are ordained by an absolute and supreme authority. This helps place at least some fundamental laws beyond challenge, thereby ensuring social stability. [Harari 2014]

Religion can thus be defined as a system of human norms and values that is founded on a belief in a superhuman order. This involves two distinct criteria: [Harari 2014]
1. Religions hold that there is a superhuman order, which is not the product of human whims or agreements.
2. Based on this superhuman order, religion establishes norms and values that it considers binding.

A religion must possess two further qualities. First, it must espouse a universal superhuman order that is true always and everywhere. Second, it must insist on spreading this belief to everyone. In other words, it must be universal and missionary. [Harari 2014]

Science and Religion

Science is not the only way to pursue knowledge and there is a confrontation between science and religion on matters affecting human nature. Human nature identifies moral knowledge too, which is the province of art, literature, and music. And just possibly there is transcendental knowledge, which is the province of religion. Why privilege science, just because it sets out to explain the world? Why not give weight to the disciplines that interpret the world and so help us to be at home in it?[Scruton 2017]

Over the last 200 years, the life sciences have thoroughly undermined religious beliefs. Scientists studying the inner workings of the human organism have found no soul in our bodies. They increasingly argue that human behavior is determined by hormones, genes, and synapses, rather than by free will – the same forces that determine the behavior of chimpanzees, wolves, and ants. However, we know that there is much more in our humanity than chemistry.

Human nature is more complex than biology, chemistry, science, religion or political systems. The way we think and act surpasses any physical limitations. Our judicial and political systems largely try to sweep such inconvenient discoveries under the carpet. But in all frankness, how long can we maintain the wall separating the department of biology from the departments of law and political science? [Harari 2014]

Myths

Myths have been a way of using the notion of superstition into modern societies. The human secret to cross the critical tribal threshold of 150 people and founding cities comprising tens of thousands of inhabitants was probably the appearance of fiction. Large numbers of strangers can cooperate successfully by believing in common myths and these myths exist only in people's collective imagination. Churches follow religious myths, states follow national myths, judicial systems follow legal myths. Yet none of these myths exist outside the stories that people invent and tell one another. [Harari 2014]

The ability to create an imagined reality out of words enabled large numbers of strangers to cooperate effectively. Large-scale human cooperation is based on myths and the way people cooperate can be altered by changing the myths – by telling different stories. Under the right circumstances, myths can change rapidly. For example, the French Revolution switched almost overnight from believing in the myth of the divine right of kings to believing in the myth of the sovereignty of the people. [Harari 2014]

The problem at the root of such calamities is that humans evolved for millions of years in small bands of a few dozen individuals. The handful of millennia separating the Agricultural Revolution from the appearance of cities, kingdoms, and empires was not enough time to allow an instinct for mass cooperation to evolve. [Harari 2014]

Despite the lack of such biological instincts, during the foraging era, hundreds of strangers were able to cooperate thanks to their shared myths. However, this cooperation was loose and limited. Every Sapiens band continued to run its life independently and to provide for most of its own needs. Modern human cooperation is relative, it is not that everybody is cooperating happily with everybody, it is that through the division of labor people can give a contribution that benefits others. Most of the time, people don't know who they are contributing to.

Myths, it transpired, are stronger than anyone could have imagined. When the Agricultural Revolution opened opportunities for the creation of crowded cities and mighty empires, people invented stories about great gods, motherlands and joint-stock companies to provide the needed social links. While human evolution was crawling at its usual snail's pace, the human imagination was building astounding networks of mass cooperation, unlike any other ever seen on earth. [Harari 2014]

<u>Coincidences are Misleading</u> (The Texas Sharpshooter Fallacy)

Coincidences are nourished by superstitions. People tend to ignore random chance when the results seem meaningful or when people want a random event to have a meaningful cause. It isn't true that people take randomness into account when determining cause and effect. [McRaney 2011]

Natural random chance is more probable than artificial order created by human's imagination. Picking out clusters of coincidence is a predictable malfunction of normal human logic. The fallacy gets its name from imagining a cowboy shooting at a barn. Over time, the side of the barn becomes riddled with holes. In some places there are lots of them, in others, there are few. If the cowboy later paints a bull's-eye over a spot where his bullet holes clustered together, it looks like he is pretty good with a gun. By painting a bull's-eye over a cluster of bullet holes, the cowboy places artificial order over natural random chance.

One of the reasons scientists form a hypothesis and then try to disprove it with new research is to avoid the Texas sharpshooter fallacy. The reach of the fallacy is far greater than reality shows, presidential trivia, and spooky coincidences. Anywhere people are searching for meaning, they will see the Texas sharpshooter fallacy. When people use the sharpshooter fallacy to determine the cause from effect, it can harm people.

To admit the messy slog of chaos, disorder, and random chance ruling our life and the universe itself is a painful conceit. People commit the Texas sharpshooter fallacy when they need a pattern to provide meaning, to console them, to lay blame. People need order. The order makes it easier to be a person, to navigate this sloppy world. For ancient man, pattern recognition led to food and protected people from harm. Evolution has made us into beings looking for clusters where chance events have built up like sand into dunes.

People see patterns everywhere, but some of them are formed by chance and mean nothing. Against the noisy background of probability, things are bound to line up from time to time for no reason at all. It's just how the math works out. Recognizing this is an important part of ignoring coincidences when they don't matter and realizing what has real meaning for people on this planet, in this epoch.

Believing Vague Statements (Subjective Validation)

Subjective validation increases with superstitions. People are prone to believe that vague statements and predictions are true, especially if they are positive and address them personally. It isn't true that people are skeptical of generalities. [McRaney 2011]

The tendency to believe vague statements designed to appeal to just about anyone is called the Forer effect and psychologists point to this phenomenon to explain why people fall for pseudosciences like biorhythms, iridology, and phrenology, or mysticism like astrology, numerology, and tarot cards. The Forer effect is part of larger phenomenon psychologists refer to as subjective validation, which is a fancy way of saying people are far more vulnerable to suggestion when the subject of the conversation is themselves.

Since people are always in their head, thoughts about what it means to be themselves take up a lot of mental space. With some cultural variations, most people are keen on being individuals, unique and special persons whose hopes and dreams and fears and doubts are all their own. If people have the means, they personalize everything: their license plate, their ring tone, their computer's desktop wallpaper, their bedroom's walls.

If a statement is ambiguous and people think it addresses them directly, they will boil away the ambiguity by finding ways to match the information up with their own traits. You think back to all the time spent figuring out who they are, dividing their qualities from the qualities of others, and applying the same logic.

Seen straight on, horoscopes describe the sort of things we all experience, but pluck one from the bunch, turn it ever so slightly, and you will see it matching all the details of your life. If you believe you live under a sign, and the movement of the planets can divine your future, a general statement becomes specific.

It is this hope that gives subjective validation its power. If people want the psychic to be real, or the sacred stones to forecast the unknown, they will find a way to believe them even when they falter. When people need something to be true, they will look for patterns; they connect the dots like the stars of a constellation. Their brain abhors disorder. They see faces in clouds and demons in bonfires. People are creatures impelled to hope. People attempting to make sense of the world focus on what falls into place and neglect that which doesn't fit, and there is so much in life that does not fit.

Ignorance Confirms nor Denies (The Argument from Ignorance)

The argument from ignorance is supported by superstitions. When people are unsure of something, they are more likely to accept strange explanations. It isn't true that when people can't explain something, they focus on what they can prove. [McRaney 2011]

It is easy to succumb to mystical thinking when people compare what they know for sure to the vast expanse of things yet unsolved. If people are not up-to-date on the latest scientific research, they put concepts like tiny seeds becoming giant plants in the realm of the unknown. Some people see things like magnets and Stonehenge as unsolvable mysteries. People tend to pattern recognition, they look for cause and effect, but when the cause is unclear they commit a logical fallacy by thinking all the possible causes are equal.

You can't disprove something you don't know anything about, and the argument-from-ignorance fallacy can make people feel as though something is possible because they can't prove otherwise. Lack of proof neither confirms nor denies a proposition. Is there life on other planets? We can't say yes or no just because it hasn't been discovered yet. It is incorrect to assume the lack of evidence proves the assumption. Things are not more likely just because you can't prove they don't exist.

People shouldn't just live their life so open-minded they never accept the proof. People who refuse to believe certain propositions claim they need more evidence before they can change their minds, but sometimes no amount of evidence will satisfy them. Any shred of doubt allows people to argue from ignorance.

<u>Miraculous Coincidences</u> (Apophenia)

Apophenia is supported by superstitions. Coincidences are a routine part of life, even the seemingly miraculous ones. Any meaning applied to them comes from people's minds. It isn't true that coincidences are miraculous and have meaning. [McRaney 2011]

Stories need a strong protagonist with whom people can identify. Early on, the protagonist will save someone without having to, and people start liking him or her. On the other side, people need a dastardly antagonist who harms someone for no reason, a person who ignores the rules and wants only to satisfy him – or herself no matter the cost.

The outline above is called the hero's journey. It is common mythology in all humans, the stories people and everyone else know in their hearts. The hero's journey is a monomyth that plugs into our mind like a key into a lock.

A certain kind of story, a mystery, plays on a type of narrative people often believe to be unfolding in the real world. When mysterious happenings are at the center of the plot, clues pop up that turn out to be connected in some strange way. People keep intrigued by the patterns slowly coalescing, to see how everything connects in the end. When it happens in the real world, it is called apophenia.

Apophenia becomes an issue only when people decide coincidences and random sorting is more than the occasional signal rising from the noise. People find it amazing when they share their birthday with a dozen celebrities, even though they share their birthday with about 16 million other people.

Math, science, and logic are harder to contemplate than social situations. People are keenly aware of what role they play and who is on the stage, it is the story of their life. The memory tends to delete the boring parts and focus on the highlights – the plot points. When people notice coincidences, they remember them and tell others. Sometimes they make their way into the news.

<u>Looking for Patterns in Chaos</u> (The Illusion of Control)

Thinking of having control of random events is influenced by superstitions. People often believe they have control over outcomes that are either random or are too complex to predict. It isn't true that people know how much control they have over their surroundings. [McRaney 2011]

In gambling, whether it be on a slot machine, a roulette table, or in a game of cards, you tend to see yourself as being lucky or unlucky, on a streak or in a rut. You say things like "The cards are about to turn." You see a change of dealers as a positive sign, or you notice when people get up from the table and change the rotation of the deal. You get two out of three cherries and decide to go for another spin; you bet on red after black comes up ten times in a row because you think red is due.

Our ancestors lived long enough to meet a partner and have children one after the other, generation upon generation, for millions of years because they were great at pattern recognition. Predators, prey, friends, and foes all stood out from the background because our kin could see signals amid the noise. Thanks to them, we've inherited the same powers, but we can't turn them off. Our brain is always looking for patterns and sending little squirts of happy throughout our body when it finds them, but like faces in clouds, we often see patterns where none exist.

Most people engage in magical thinking to some degree, assuming their thoughts can influence things outside of their control. The people in the experiments knew they were in a study, so they likely were more skeptical than usual. This skepticism can dissolve away in the right conditions. If you are an avid sports fan, you can't help but think your mental cheerleading has some sort of positive effect on the gameplay. You take some credit when your team wins. You think you didn't cheer hard enough if they lose. This illusion of control is pervasive enough to show up when teachers take credit for the success of their students or people in war zones start to accumulate lucky charms or engage in rituals they think will keep them alive. You ask people to send well wishes and positive thoughts when someone is sick.

Psychologists point out these findings do not suggest people should throw up their hands and give up. Those who are not grounded in reality, oddly enough, often achieve a lot in life simply because they believe they can and try harder than others. If people focus too long on their lack of power, they can slip into a state of learned helplessness that will whirl them into a negative feedback loop of depression. Some control is necessary or else people give up altogether.

Knowing about the illusion of control shouldn't discourage you from attempting to carve a space for yourself out of whatever field you want to tackle. After all, doing nothing guarantees no results. But as you do so, remember most of the future is unforeseeable. Learn to coexist with chaos. Factor it into your plans. Accept that failure is always a possibility, even if you are one of the good guys; those who believe failure is not an option never plan for it.

Chapter 14: Responsibility

The feature of responsibility is another characteristic related to human nature. We hold each other accountable for what we do, and as a result, we understand the world in ways that have no parallel in the lives of other species. Our world, unlike the environment of an animal, contains rights, deserts, and duties; it is a world of self-conscious subjects, in which events are divided into the free and the unfree, those that have reasons and those that are merely caused, those that stem from a rational subject and those that erupt into the stream of objects with no conscious design.[Scruton 2017]

It is interesting to recognize that people would like to do whatever they want without any interference. People do not like to be accountable for what they do. Maturity makes people understand that anything they do is observed by others and there are consequences for their decisions. Immature people always complain about this constant interference in their own affairs. Society should prepare people to adapt to possible interference and help regulate misbehavior towards better comprehension and empathy.

<u>Obligation and Choice</u>

For humans, who enter a world marked by the joys and sufferings of those who are making room for us, who enjoy protection in our early years and opportunities in our maturity, the field of obligation is wider than the field of choice. We are bound by ties that we never chose, and our world contains values and challenges that intrude from beyond the comfortable arena of our agreements. In the attempt to encompass these values and challenges, human beings have developed concepts that have little or no place in liberal theories of the social contract – concepts of the sacred and the sublime, of evil and redemption, that suggest a completely different orientation to the world than that assumed by modern moral philosophy. [Scruton 2017]

Filial obligations provide a clear example. I did not consent to be born from and raised by my mom. I have not bound myself to her by a contract, and there is no knowing in advance what my obligation to her at any point might be or what might fulfill it. The Confucian philosophy places enormous weight on obligations of this kind – obligations of li – and regards a person's virtue measured almost entirely on the scale of piety.

The ability to recognize and act upon unchosen obligations indicates a character more deeply imbued with a trustworthy feeling than the ability to make deals and bide by them – such is the thought. [Scruton 2017]

When the fault is ours we blame ourselves, and good people blame themselves more severely than others would. We recognize obligations to those that depend on us and on whom we depend, and we exist at the center of the sphere of accountability, which stretches out from us with dwindling force across the world of other people. [Scruton 2017]

It would be fair to say that the main task of political conservatism was to put obligations of piety back where they belong, at the center of the picture. And they were right to undertake this task. One thing that is unacceptable in the political philosophies that compete for our endorsement today is their failure to recognize that most of what we are and owe has been acquired without our own consent to it. In Hegel's Philosophy of Right, the family is defined as a sphere of pious obligations, and civil society, as a sphere of free choice and contract; the destiny of political order and the destiny of the family are connected. Families, and the relationships embraced by them are nonaccidental features of interpersonal life, just like the experiences of pollution and violation. [Scruton 2017]

<u>Interpreting Responsibility</u>

Like any other behavioral characteristic, responsibility depends on the context and the interpretation of the duties. Responsibility is the state or fact of having a duty to deal with something or having to establish control over someone. Establishing the context and interpretation of responsibility is a task that requires intelligence and comprehension. There is an interesting contrast between two possible readings of Christ's parable of the Good Samaritan, given in answer to the question "Who is my neighbor?"

The orthodox reading tells us that Christ was telling us to ignore distinctions of ethnicity and faith and to do good to others in an impartial and universal way. ... a consequentialist morality, which advocates optimal solutions to our moral dilemmas and ignores those historically incurred obligations that cause us to distinguish between people and communities. But there is another and more plausible reading, according to which the Samaritan finds himself confronted with a specific obligation to a specific person. His assistance is offered in response to an individual need; it is not a contribution to the sum of the good but an obligation to a fellow human being who is appealing immediately for help. On this second reading of the parable, the moral life is represented as rooted in personal obligations. [Scruton 2017]

Should versus Want (Procrastination)

Procrastination enters the realm of responsibility. It is fueled by weakness in the face of impulse and a failure to think about thinking. It isn't true that procrastination is a well-known defect in humans and that people don't start certain tasks or don't finish some other activities because of a natural propensity to leave things for later. It isn't true that people procrastinate because they are lazy and can't manage their time well. [McRaney 2011]

Many studies over the years have shown people tend to have time-inconsistent preferences. When asked if they would rather have healthy food or junk food a week from now, people will usually say healthy food. A week later, however, when the slice of sweet chocolate cake and the grapes are offered, people are statistically more likely to go for the cake.

For example, people that read articles on the internet about specific subjects, such as psychology, astronomy, science, and so on, keep storing files for future reading; the memory space in the computer begins to grow and grow and they never start reading the articles. Why don't they read them? Basically, the answer is that people tend to be good at planning for the future but in the present, they choose differently. This is called present bias – being unable to grasp that what people want will change over time, and what they want now isn't the same thing they will want later. Present bias is why people make resolutions at the beginning of the year, and they mean them, but never accomplish them at the end of the year.

Procrastination manifests itself within every aspect of people's life. Waiting to the last minute to filing taxes, or washing the car, or going for a walk with the family dog. People think they will get around it, that they will do it the next day. However, before starting, maybe check the email first, or go for a cup of coffee, or watch the basketball game.

Self-control is fundamental to overcome desires for short-term rewards in favor of better outcomes later. Self-control allows people to have a better grasp of how to trick themselves into doing what is best for them. The ones who are better at holding off their frivolous desires use the same power to squeeze more out of life. The ones who could not hold off their desires show a higher incidence of behavioral problems.

Faced with two possible rewards, people are more likely to take the one that can be enjoyed now over the one to be enjoyed later – even if the later reward is far greater. Doing something at the moment that may seem a lot more rewarding than some other task due in future weeks which might affect family or job relationships, people wait until the night before to do the latter. However, if people considered more valuable the task due in the future weeks they would pick the greater reward. The tendency to get more rational when people are forced to wait is called hyperbolic discounting because the dismissal of the better payoff later diminished over time.

<u>Influenced by Others</u> (The Bystander Effect)

The bystander effect is fueled by a misinterpretation of responsibility where the group becomes unresponsive. The more people who witness a person in distress, the less likely it is that anyone person will help. It isn't true that when someone is hurt, people rush to their aid. [McRaney 2011]

Have you ever seen someone broken down on the side of the road and thought, "I could help them, but I'm sure someone will be along." Everyone thinks that. And no one stops. This is called the bystander effect.

In a crowd, your inclination to rush to someone's aid fades, as if diluted by the potential of the group. Everyone thinks someone is going to eventually do something, but with everyone waiting together, no one does.

Social psychologists started studying the bystander effect soon after a story of a woman being stabbed went viral, and they determined that the more people present when a person needs emergency help, the less likely it is any one of them will lend a hand.

The findings suggest the fear of embarrassment plays into group dynamics. People see the smoke in the room, but they don't want to look like a fool, so they glance over at the other persons to see what they are doing. The other persons are thinking about the same thing. Neither one reacts, so neither one becomes alarmed. The third person sees two people acting like everything is OK, so that the third person is even less likely to freak out.

If an individual were to walk along a bridge and see someone in the water screaming for help, he would feel a much greater urge to leap in and pull them to safety than somebody would if he were part of a crowd. When it's just one person, all the responsibility to help is his. The bystander effect gets stronger when people think the person who needs help is being harmed by someone that person knows. It takes only one person to help others to join in.

Chapter 15: Reality versus Fantasy

We are seldom what we make ourselves out to be. And this may be both good news and bad news. Perhaps we are not the meek and gentle person we thought we were. Perhaps we have great reservoirs of willpower and even ruthlessness, given the right project. Perhaps we are both more and less than we thought. But, even given the potential disappointment, is it not better to become who we are than to be someone else? [Huenemann 2009]

How do we separate fantasy from reality? How can we be sure the story of our life both from long ago and minute to minute is true? There is a pleasant vindication to be found when people accept they can't. No one can, yet we persist and thrive. How people think they live is sort of like a movie based on true events, which is not necessarily a bad thing. The details may be embellished, but the big picture, the general idea, is probably a good story worth hearing about.

Human beings are usually deluded regarding reality and fantasy. Humans invent stories to cope with harsh reality. Fantasy is in most cases unattainable, and people must be clear that dreams usually don't come true. However, it is healthy to believe in fantasy and keep striving with some hope than to surrender to reality and stop struggling in life. As we evaluate ourselves and others, the question is whether we will judge the fantasy or the psychological reality. Sticking to fantasy will only perpetuate the illusions. Facing reality will lead to genuine transformation. [Huenemann 2009]

There are many considerations surrounding experiences. The characters involved and the context of the experience are important aspects. Any given experience may be interpreted in many ways, and widely varying conclusions can be drawn from it. Characters are subject to personality issues and each character combined with the context provides multiple interpretations and views. For example, fifty years ago teenagers lived in a different world compared to today and it is unclear whether the world we live in today is better than the world ten thousand years ago; a person with behavioral disorders cannot be compared to one behaving normally; an old man who has struggled to succeed during his life is a better source of advice than somebody that didn't do much. People turn, twist and distort their experiences to fit into their behavioral patterns. It is common practice to forget about the context of experiences. [Adler 1992]

Fictional narratives (Confabulation)

Confabulation is created by the misunderstanding between reality and fantasy. People are often ignorant of their motivations and create fictional narratives to explain their decisions, emotions, and history without realizing it. It isn't true that people know when they are lying to themselves. [McRaney 2011]

Think of all the photographs that have blown your mind when you saw yourself in a place you had completely deleted from memory. Think of all the things your parents bring back up about your childhood that you have zero recollection of, or which you remember differently. But you still have a sense of a continuous memory and experience. The details are missing, but the big picture of your own life persists. But the big picture is a lie, nurtured by your constant and unconscious confabulation, adding up to a story of who you are, what you have done, and why.

People are confabulatory creatures by nature. People are always explaining to themselves the motivations for their actions and the causes of the effects in their life, and people make them up without realizing it when they don't know the answers. Over time, these explanations become the idea of who they are and their place in the world. The explanations define people themselves. People are a story they tell themselves. People engage in introspection, and with great confidence, they see the history of their life with all the characters and settings – and they at the center as the protagonist in the tale of who they are. This is all a great, beautiful confabulation without which people could not function.

How people's minds works is something they can never access, and although people often believe they understand their thoughts and actions, their emotions and motivations, much of the time they don't. The very act of looking inward is already several steps removed from the thoughts people are remembering. This, however, doesn't prevent people from assuming they do know, that they really can recall in full detail, and this is how narratives begin. This is how confabulation provides a framework from which to understand themselves.

"It is the result of thinking, not the process of thinking, that appears spontaneously in consciousness." In other words, people are only reporting on what their mind has already produced instead of directing its performance. The flow of consciousness is one thing; the recollection of its course is another, yet people usually see them as the same.

Imagined World (The Just-World Fallacy)

The just-world fallacy is fueled by our misunderstanding of reality. It establishes that the beneficiaries of good fortune often do nothing to earn it, and bad people often get away with their actions without consequences. However, it isn't true that people who are losing at the game of life must have done something wrong to deserve it. [McRaney 2011]

If we think the world is just and fair, people who need help may never get it. Just remember the unfair nature of the world, the randomness of birthright means people enjoy opulence through no effort of their own while others often suffer adversity. It is common in fiction for the bad guys to lose and the good guys to win. This is how people would like to see the world – just and fair. Success is often greatly influenced by when people were born, where they grew up, the socioeconomic status of their family, and random chance. All the hard work in the world can't change those initial factors. Accepting this does not mean those born poor should just give up.

The real world is more complicated. People can and do escape, but this doesn't mean those who haven't aren't trying their damnedest to claw out of bad situations. If people look to the downtrodden and wonder why they can't pull themselves out of poverty and get a nice job like others, they are committing the just-world fallacy. They are ignoring the unearned blessings of their station. After all, not taking action guarantees not getting results. In a just world, this would be the only rule, no matter what the initial conditions of our struggle are.

It is infuriating when cheats and con politicians get ahead in the world while firemen and policemen put in long hours for little pay. Deep down, you want to believe hard work and virtue will lead to success, and evil and manipulation will lead to ruin, so people go ahead and edit the world to match those expectations. Yet, in reality, evil often prospers and never pays the price. Realize that even though we are all responsible for our actions, the blame for evil acts rests on the perpetrator and never the victim. No one deserves to be bullied, robbed or murdered.

Willing is Believing (Self-Fulfilling Prophecies)

Self-fulfilling prophecies are fueled by reality considerations. Just believing a future event will happen can cause it to happen if the event depends on human behavior. It isn't true that predictions about people's futures are subject to forces beyond their control. [McRaney 2011]

Self-fulfilling prophecies gain their power from social definitions of reality, and most of the people's life is defined socially, not logically. If the perceptions of others translate into actions, policies, and beliefs, the perceptions become reality simply because so much of life is ruled by behavior.

Without scientific analysis, ideas like bottled water are better than tap water can go from true to false to maybe and back again because they are socially defined. They depend on subjective feelings and a vacillating consensus of beliefs. People swim in a sea of social ideas and mental constructs shared by culture both ancient and popular.

The initial phase of a self-fulfilling prophecy is always a false interpretation of an ongoing situation. The behavior that follows assumes the situation is real, and when enough people act as if something is real it can sometimes make it so. What was once false becomes true, and in hindsight, it seems as if it always was.

Research shows people are highly susceptible to self-fulfilling prophecies because they are always trying to predict the behavior of others. The easiest example of this is the rumor of a shortage. If you believe there will be a shortage of toothpaste, you will go and try to buy some before the stores run out – just like everyone else. Sure enough, the shortage occurs. The self-fulfilling prophecy is a concept that goes far back into the history of storytelling and narrative fiction in just about all human cultures, but it isn't fiction.

In social psychology, a version of the self-fulfilling prophecy called labeling theory shows how when someone believes you are a certain kind of person, you tend to live up to those expectations. For example, if your teacher thinks you are smart, the teacher treats you like a smart person. You get extra attention and respect. You react with more effort, more drive, and the positive feedback loop leads to the fulfillment of your label.

Think of the stock market. When people predict it will fail, they stop investing and start selling. Others hear about the selling, and they sell. People start to try and predict the future, assume everyone is going to sell, and they sell too. Once the media starts reporting, stocks plummet.

Stories versus Statistics (The Availability Heuristic)

The availability heuristic is related to fantasy and reality considerations. People are far more likely to believe something is commonplace if they can find one example of it, and they are far less likely to believe in something they have never seen or heard before. It isn't true that with the advent of mass media people understand how the world works based on statistics and facts culled from many examples. [McRaney 2011]

If someone you know gets sick from taking a flu shot, you will be less likely to get one even if it is statistically safe. If you see a story on the news about someone dying from the flu shot, that one isolated case could be enough to keep you away from the vaccine forever. On the other hand, if you hear a news story about how eating sausage leads to brain cancer, you will be skeptical, because it has never happened to anyone you know, and sausage, after all, is delicious. The tendency to react more rapidly and to a greater degree when considering the information you are familiar with is called the availability heuristic. The adage "I'll believe it when I see it" is the availability heuristic at work.

Politicians use this all the time. Whenever you hear a story that begins with "I met a mother of two in Michigan who lost her job because of a lack of funding for . . ." or something similar, the politician hopes the anecdote will sway your opinion. He or she is betting that the availability heuristic will influence you to assume that this one example is indicative of a much larger group of people. It's simply easier to believe something if you are presented with examples than it is to accept something presented in numbers or abstract facts.

Chapter 16: Egocentricity

Humans are primarily egocentrics and they have no choice. Humans tend to see things according to their viewpoint at first and then, after some reflection, they may consider the point of view of others. To survive in life, people must struggle and must do the effort of living; first, by their effort and next sharing efforts with others. Even though egocentric is related to egotism, it is the inexorable condition of living with themselves that makes humans revolve around their ego.

Egotism and egoism are related, even though they are not the same, one considers that self-interest is the actual motive of all conscious action whilst the other describes people who are full of themselves and don't care about others. Egoism is a doctrine that establishes individual self-interest as the actual motive of all conscious actions. Egoism is also an excessive concern for oneself with or without exaggerated feelings of self-importance. Egotism includes the practice of talking about oneself too much. Both terms describe a conscious decision-making process compared to egocentrics, an innate characteristic.

<u>Egocentric Appreciation</u> (Self-serving Bias)

Self-serving bias is fueled by egocentric instincts. People use to have a positive appreciation of themselves that tends to be overly exaggerated. They don't objectively evaluate themselves using facts. Since childhood, people are subject to a bombardment of criteria to be above average. People see themselves as more successful, more intelligent, and more skilled than they are. It is not true that people are evaluating themselves based on past successes and defeats. [McRaney 2011]

People don't evaluate themselves based on past successes and defeats, they are egocentric, they see their performance as superior to anybody else. If people were to stop and truly examine their faults and failures, they would become paralyzed by fear and doubt. Self-esteem is mostly self-delusion but it serves a purpose, to avoid stagnation. Self-esteem is convenient for survival, however, the tendency to see ourselves as an above average is not appropriate.

Comparing themselves to others, people feel more competent than their coworkers, more ethical than their friends, friendlier than the general public, more intelligent than their peers, and more attractive than the average person. People don't believe they are average persons but they believe everyone else is. If people never see how much they are screwing up their life, mistreating their spouses and friends, and being completely obnoxious, they can destroy themselves without realizing how bad things have become. They might see their past-person as a foolish incompetent with poor taste but their current person as an intimidating personage who is worthy of at least three times the praise.

People tend to accept credit when they succeed but blame bad luck when they don't. When they are doing well, they think they are the ones to praise and when they are doing badly, they think the world is to be blamed. When they fail, they blame unfair rules, difficult instructors, bad bosses, cheaters, and so on.

Current and Remembering Self (The Moment)

The actual moment and the past are remembered differently. People are multiple selves, and happiness is based on satisfying all of them. It isn't true that people are one person, and their happiness is based on being content with their life. [McRaney 2011]

To understand the difference between experience and memory, people first need to understand a little bit about themselves. The sense of self is just that – a sense. The person we imagine ourselves to be is a story we tell to ourselves and others differently depending on the situation, and the story changes over time. It is useful to imagine there are two selves active at any given time in your head – the current self and the remembering self.

The current self is the one experiencing life in real-time. It is the person we are in the three or so seconds our sensory memory lasts, and the thirty or so seconds after that in which our short-term memory is juggling all our senses and thoughts. We taste the ice cream and it is good, then, we remember we tasted the ice cream. Then, after a while, we have no memory of tasting it at all. Sometimes, rarely, something happens and we move it to long-term storage.

When we replay our life in our minds, we can't go back to all the things we have ever experienced. Only the things that went from experience to short-term memory to long-term memory are available to fully remember. Going to drink a coffee is not about building awesome memories. It's about being happy for a few minutes. It's about gratification. The happiness derived from such an experience is fleeting.

The self that makes decisions in people's life is usually the remembering one. It drags the current self around in pursuit of new memories, anticipating them based on old memories. The current self has little control over the future. It can control only a few actions, like moving a hand away from a hot stove or putting one foot in front of the other. Occasionally, it prompts people to eat a cheeseburger, or watch a horror movie, or play a video game. The current self is happy when experiencing things. It likes to be in the flow.

Important People (The Representativeness Heuristic)

The representativeness heuristic is an egocentric misinterpretation of reality. People jump to conclusions based on how representative a person seems to be of a preconceived character type. It's not the person's history that makes it easier to determine what sort of person a person is, it is what he represents that matter. [McRaney 2011]

Unless people have spent time as a therapist, chances are they don't know a lot about people who are different from them. For everyone else, people haul around prejudices, some benign, some less so. Prejudices help people think faster, to build models of the unknown in a way that allows them to make decisions effortlessly.

Categories are a great way to make sense of things. Without filters, the world around people is chaos. Over time people develop shortcuts to cognition. When it comes to strangers, people's first instinct is to fit them into archetypes to quickly determine their value or threat. These constructs are called the representativeness heuristic.

The conjunction fallacy is the assumption that more specific conditions are more probable than general ones, and it builds on our representativeness heuristic. The more things people hear about which match their mental models, the more likely they seem.

People don't naturally think in statistical, logical, rational terms. People first go to their emotional core and think of people in terms of narratives and characters that match their preconceived notions of the sort of people they have been exposed to in the past or have imagined thanks to cultural osmosis.

Representativeness heuristics are useful, but also dangerous. They can help people avoid danger and seek help, but they can also lead to generalizations and prejudices. Their mental models aren't accurate, nor do they usually need to be. They just need to pop right into their minds automatically and without effort.

The Person is the Message (The Argument from Authority)

The argument from authority is an egocentric misinterpretation of what someone represents. The status and credentials of an individual greatly influence their perception of that individual's message. It isn't true that people are more concerned with the validity of information than the person delivering it. [McRaney 2011]

A professor of history will likely know why the Soviet Union fell and what can be learned from it than someone who pretends to know. Those who devote their lives to the study or practice of a given idea are worth listening to when it comes to the areas of their expertise, but this doesn't mean all their opinions are golden. When he or she opines on the physics of the universe, you might be inclined to see the professor's point of view as more correct, more thoroughly meditated upon than someone else who has not read a book in his life. Beware.

If a professor tells you how sure he is about God being alive, it would be a logical fallacy if you decided you should maybe rethink your atheist's beliefs. When people see the opinions of some people as better than others on the merit of their status or training alone, they are arguing from authority. Should you listen to a highly trained electrician's advice before changing the power electrical panel? Yes. Should you believe that person when he talks about becoming more intelligent after receiving a few electrical discharges in his brain? No.

Looking for the consensus of scientists on certain behaviors is a way to prove how deluded people are on certain matters. Science focuses on the facts, not the people who unearth them, therefore, it is better to believe in scientific facts. It is not a fallacy to trust the consensus of thousands of researchers on how to interpret the evidence provided by decades of studies. However, that doesn't mean that large groups of people can't agree on something wrong, therefore, be always cautious of scientific research.

If people feel more inclined to believe something is true because it comes from a person with prestige, they are letting the argument from authority spin their head. If something is controversial, it usually means many experts disagree. They would be wise to come to their conclusions based on the evidence, and not on believing the people delivering it. On the other hand, if there is widespread consensus, they can relax their skepticism. Just don't relax completely.

Center of attention (The Spotlight Effect)

The spotlight effect is an egocentric view of ourselves. People devote little attention to others unless they are prompted to. It isn't true that when around others, people are noticing every aspect of their appearance and behavior. [McRaney 2011]

People can't help but be the center of the universe, and they find it difficult to gauge just how much other people are paying attention since they are paying attention to themselves all the time. When people spend so much time thinking about their own body, their thoughts, and behaviors, they begin to think other people must be noticing too. The research says they aren't, at least not nearly as much as people think.

The spotlight effect was studied to determine the degree to which people believe their actions and appearance are noticed by others. While doing an activity, people feel like everyone else is keeping up with how good they are doing. The spotlight effect is strong for both positive and negative images of oneself, but the real world is far less likely to give a damn when people are trying to look cool.

Research shows people believe others see their contributions to the conversation as being memorable, but they aren't. People think everyone noticed when they stumbled in their speech, but almost nobody did. Well, unless people drew attention to it by over-apologizing.

Accepting and Conforming (Conformity)

Conformity is an egocentric characteristic that makes us yield. It takes little more than an authority figure or social pressure to get people to obey because conformity is a survival instinct. It isn't true that people are strong individuals who don't conform unless forced to. [McRaney 2011]

There is too much conformity in life. Sometimes is an innate attribute, other times is an imposed attribute. However, humans must keep in mind that they are surrounded by myth and myth is a human invention. Only too many human beings have acquired the habit of accepting authority without testing it. The public wants to be fooled. It wants to swallow every tall story whole without subjecting it to rational examination. The revolt of those who have been deceived would be the answer. [Adler 1992]

People are often not even aware of when they are conforming. It is their home base, their default mode. People conform because social acceptance is built into their brains. To thrive, people know they need allies. People get a better picture of the world when they can receive information from multiple sources. People need friends because outcasts are cut off from valuable resources.

Be aware: our desire to conform is strong and unconscious. People should never be afraid to question authority when their actions could harm themselves or others. Even in simple situations, like the next time they see a line of people waiting to get into a classroom or a movie or a restaurant, feel free to break norms – go check the door and look inside.

What happens in a group trying to get consensus. Most of the time, people try to conform to the group and accept the unacceptable. Sometimes agreeing to something wrong, just to go with the group.

<u>Reframing Arguments</u> (The Straw Man Fallacy)

The straw man fallacy is an egocentric position of superiority to manipulate others. In any argument, anger will tempt people to reframe their opponent's position. It isn't true that when people argue, they try to stick to the facts. [McRaney 2011]

When people are losing an argument, they often use a variety of deceptive techniques to bolster their opinion. They aren't trying to be sneaky, but the human mind tends to follow predictable patterns when they get angry with other people and do battle with words. One of the most reliable and sturdy logical fallacies is the straw man, and even though its probability of appearing is high, people often don't notice when they are using it or being beat over the head with it.

It works like this: When people get into an argument about either something personal or something more public and abstract, they sometimes resort to constructing a character who they find easier to refute, argue, and disagree with, or they create a position the other person isn't even suggesting or defending. This is a straw man construct.

It happens so often, professional debaters and science advocates are trained to look for the straw man fallacy both in themselves and opponents when asserting their opinions or shooting down the claims of others. The straw man fallacy takes the facts and assertions of your opponent and replaces them with an artificial argument you feel more comfortable dealing with.

The straw man fallacy follows a familiar pattern. First, build the straw man, then attack it, then point out how easy it was to defeat it, and then come to a conclusion. Pay attention the next time people disagree with someone, and see if they start or the other person starts to construct a man out of straw. Keep in mind whoever does it is using a logical fallacy, and even if that person succeeds, he or she didn't win.

Chapter 17: Judging

Judgment, both conscious and unconscious, is a fundamental part of the human experience. People do it around the clock because it's a necessary function of moving, acting, and living in a dynamic world. And while people can't do much about the beliefs they form without conscious participation, they design their systems of how to evaluate others. The two most commonly 'taught' approaches on how people interact with others are: one based on actions, the other based on intentions.

When you grow up in an environment where little emphasis is placed on outcomes, where you feel that your best is always good enough, chances are, you will hold others mostly to their intentions too. If you're raised under the motto of "actions speak louder than words," however, it's usually the result that matters. Both systems have their advantages and disadvantages, so it's hard to declare one superior to the other. Placing importance on intentions allows you to be patient and kind while focusing on actions is a great motivator to try hard and hold both people and yourself accountable.

The connection between morality and religion is not an accident, as persons, we make ourselves accountable for our actions and states of mind. Hence, even when we are unobserved, we are judged. The very habit of finding reasons that would justify us in others' eyes leads us to demand such reasons for ourselves. When asking people why they do what they do or why they like or don't like things, they must translate from a deep, emotional, primal part of their psyche into the language of the higher, logical, rational world of words and sentences and paragraphs. The awareness of our faults can weigh us down: we seek exoneration and are often remorseful, without knowing the human person to whom an appeal for forgiveness can be made. [Scruton 2017]

Human reasoning, experience, and knowledge are sustained by science and pragmatic ethics judging the consequences of actions by the well-being of humans and other species on Earth and the universe. Moreover, human societies are not just groups of cooperating primates: they are communities of persons, who live in mutual judgment, organizing their world in terms of moral concepts that arguably have no place in the thoughts of chimpanzees. [Scruton 2017]

Our brains are wired to make automatic judgments about others' behaviors so that we can move through the world without spending too much time or energy on understanding everything we see. Judge character has been such a useful tool for so long in the evolutionary history of human beings that it can overshadow people's logic.

People might be great judges of character, but they need to be great judges of evidence to avoid delusion. The only way we can understand why people act the way they do is by assembling evidence of the context in which they acted. Was their choice one they made voluntarily? Or one they were forced to make? Or maybe one they *felt* they were forced to make, even if it wasn't so?

It is a useful exercise to give others the benefit of the doubt by thinking about their situation, rather than jumping to personality characteristics, but there are limitations to this approach. Psychologists know most behavior is the result of a tug-of-war between external and internal forces. People do not always have the time to get to know other's situations, so making personality judgments tends to be quicker and more automatic, even if those types of judgments are less ideal.

This seems like common sense, but people easily forget about the power of the setting when judging others. People aren't characters without nuance who can be easily predicted. People seem a different person at work than at home, a different character at a party than when they are with their family. Instead of saying, "Jack is uncomfortable around people he doesn't know, thus when I see him in public places he tends to avoid crowds," people say, "Jack is shy." It's a shortcut, an easier way to navigate the social world.

<u>Judging the Person</u> (The Ad Hominem Fallacy)

The ad hominem fallacy is a way of judging the person instead of the idea. What someone says and why they say it should be judged separately. It isn't true that if people can't trust someone, they wouldn't ignore that person's claims. [McRaney 2011]

Sometimes an argument can get so heated you start calling the other person names. People attack other persons instead of the position those persons have taken. It is easier to disagree with someone people see as nasty or ignorant. Calling someone a bigot, or an idiot or an asshole feels good, but it does not prove you right or the other person wrong.

This makes sense, but people don't always notice when they are doing it. When people assume someone is incorrect based on who that person is or what group he or she belongs to, they have committed the ad hominem fallacy. Ad hominem is Latin for "to the person," which is where people sometimes take the argument when things get out of hand. Guilt by association is often the ad hominem fallacy at work. If someone hangs out with crooks or crazies, maybe that person is a criminal or a lunatic. A politician's policies and the people he or she barbecues with are separate issues.

People tend to see others as characters and look for consistency in their behavior. This is usually a good thing, as it helps people sort out who they can trust. Wondering whether or not someone can be trusted and wondering whether or not someone is telling the truth are two different things. The judging of character has been such a useful tool for so long in the evolutionary history of human beings it can overshadow people's logic. People might be a great judge of character, but they need to be great judges of evidence to avoid delusion.

Impact on Others (The Third Person Effect)

The third-person effect is a way of judging to defend others. People believe their opinions and decisions are based on experience and facts, while those who disagree with them are falling for the lies and propaganda of sources people don't trust. However, the truth is that everyone believes the people they disagree with are gullible, and everyone thinks they are far less susceptible to persuasion than they truly are. [McRaney 2011]

A great many messages among the countless ones bombarding people every day are considered dangerous because they might sway other people or fester in their minds until they act out on the suggestions coming out of all manner of sources, from violent video games to late-night pundit programming. For every outlet of information, some see it as dangerous not because it affects them, but because it might affect the thoughts and opinions of an imaginary third party. This sense of alarm about the impact of speech not on yourself but others is called the third-person effect.

I can see right through that politician's lies. People are such sheep. People are so stupid. People will believe anything. I prefer to lead, not to follow. Have you ever thought like this? Would it blow your mind to know everyone thinks like this? If we all think we aren't gullible and can't be swayed by advertising, political rhetoric, or charismatic con artists, then some of us must be deluding ourselves. Sometimes that's ourselves.

As modern humans, we are bombarded with media messages, but we see ourselves as less affected than others. Somehow we have been inoculated against the persuaders, we think, so we have nothing to worry about. People can't count on everyone else to be as strong as they are, so if they are like most people, there are some voices they think should be quiet. They might even go so far as to think some messages should be censored – not for them, but others.

Who are the others? It might be children, or high school kids, or college students. It might be liberals or conservatives. It might be the elderly, the middle-class, the super-rich. Whatever groups people don't belong to become the groups who they think will be bowled over by messages they don't agree with. Some people see certain messages in the media as a call to action, not because of what is being said, but because of who might hear it. Pointing to the third-person effect as the source of outrage from religious leaders over "heretical propaganda" and the ire of political rulers over some speech out of a "fear of dissent."

Self-Expectation (The Dunning-Kruger Effect)

The Dunning-Kruger effect is a judgment mechanism to defend ourselves. People are generally pretty bad at estimating their competence and the difficulty of complex tasks. It isn't true that people can predict how well they would perform in any situation. [McRaney 2011]

"The stupids are cocksure while the intelligent are full of doubts." People are not very good at estimating their competence. On easy tasks, where there is a positive bias, the best performers are also the most accurate in estimating their standing, but in difficult tasks, where there is a negative bias, the worst performers are the most accurate.

The more skilled people are the more practice they have put in it, and the fewer experiences they have, the worst they are at comparing themselves to others on certain tasks. "Ignorance more frequently gives rise to confidence than does knowledge."

Evaluation is as much about learning what people don't know as it is about adding to what they do. Amateurs are far more likely to think they are experts than actual experts are. The progression of experiences follows a well-known pattern: novice – amateur – expert – master. Being honest with ourselves and recognizing all our faults and weaknesses is not a pleasant way to live. Feeling inadequate or incompetent is paralyzing.

Context-oriented Judgment (The Attribution Error)

The attribution error is a judging mechanism that forgets the context. Other people's behavior is more the result of the situation than their disposition. It isn't true that other people's behavior is the reflection of their personality. [McRaney 2011]

When we don't know much about a person, when we haven't had a chance to get to know him or her, we tend to turn the person into a character. We lean on archetypes and stereotypes culled from experience and fantasy. Even though we know better, we still do it. We put on and take off social masks all the time. We are a different person with our friends than we are with our family or our boss. Somehow, we forget that our friends, family, and boss are doing the same.

People perpetuate the fundamental attribution error just about every time they read a news story. For instance, every once in awhile, someone snaps and goes on a killing spree at the post office. Going back to 1983, there has been a shooting near or in a U.S. post office about every two years. Often, the killer is a disgruntled employee. Sometimes they still work for the United States Postal Service, sometimes they are recently fired. There's even a phrase for the phenomenon: "going postal."

When people hear about a shooting like those at the post office or in a school or at an airport, what is the first thing people assume about the killer? The most comforting thought is that the murderer was crazy. He or she was nuts, and one day something just came over that person. In its dark way, this is comforting. People don't want to think potential killers are all around, or that anyone could lose it in such a grand and total way.

When people see the behavior of a child screaming in a supermarket while the seemingly oblivious parents continue to shop, they take a mental shortcut and conclude something about the story of that family. Even though people know they don't have enough information to understand, their conclusion still feels satisfying. Our attribution, the cause we believe to have preceded the effect, could be right on the money. Often, though, people are wrong.

People commit the fundamental attribution error by believing other people's actions burgeon from the sort of people they are and have nothing to do with the settings. When a man believes the stripper likes him, or when the boss thinks all his employees love to hear his stories about fishing in Niagara Falls, that's the fundamental attribution error.

Chapter 18: Unusual Reactions

Humans are the most bizarre creatures in the animal kingdom. The proof is in the many gross, unnecessary, contradictory and simply inexplicable things they do. And humans are different in their capacity to ponder all these oddities even though sometimes figure a few out. Humans tend to react to their environment and others in strange ways, their behavior is not predetermined and the context is fundamental.

There are so many reactions people do that the list would not fit the length of this book. To give a glimpse of these reactions, only a small sample has been chosen: lies, gossip, boredom, laughter. Some conditioned responses such as Inaction in Crisis, Excuses to Limit Failure, Pessimism Prevailing, Venting Increasing Aggression, and Overstimulation are presented.

<u>Lies</u>

People lie. They do it for many reasons (some malicious and others completely benign), but everybody lies sometimes. Lying is common and is likely linked to several psychological factors. Foremost among these factors is self-esteem. When a person's self-esteem is threatened, he or she will immediately begin to lie at different levels.

We're trying not so much to impress other people but to maintain a view of ourselves that is consistent with the way they would like us to be. In other words, people often lie to make social situations easier. This might mean telling a lie to avoid hurting someone else's feelings or to avoid a disagreement. But bald-faced lies (i.e. making something up or falsifying information) often occur when people are trying to avoid punishment or embarrassment.

<u>Gossip</u>

If you're like most humans, then you've probably been on at least one end of the grapevine a few times. Like it or not, gossip is a part of everyday life. Scientists speculate that gossip may bring humans closer together. Sometimes through gossip, people invent stories about other people and it is difficult to separate invented gossip from reality. To find out the truth, the only way is to confront the different parties and come up with clarifications.

Gossip is like the constant grooming of other primates. Baboons pick bugs out of each other's back hair; we humans talk about others behind their backs. It's the verbal glue that keeps our social bonds strong. Sharing our dislikes of others helps develop a bond between the gossiper and the listener.

Boredom

Everybody gets bored sometimes. But, if you think about it, feelings of boredom are pretty strange. After all, there's a whole wide world full of stuff to do. How could humans ever lack for something to keep us occupied?

It turns out that boredom isn't really about keeping people busy. Boredom stems from an objective lack of neurological excitement, which brings about a subjective psychological state of dissatisfaction, frustration or disinterest, according to researchers who study this yawn-inducing subject.

Laughter

Consider one of those features of people that set them apart from other species: laughter. No other animal laughs. ... To be real it would have to be an expression of amusement – laughter at something, founded in a complex pattern of thought. ... But what is amusement? No philosopher, it seems to me, has ever quite put a finger on it. [Scruton 2017]

Contrary to folk wisdom, most laughter is not about humor; it is about relationships between people. When we laugh, we're often communicating playful intent. So laughter has a bonding function within individuals in a group. It's often positive, but it can be negative too. There's a difference between "laughing with" and "laughing at." People who laugh at others may be trying to force them to conform or casting them out of the group.

Many researchers believe that the purpose of laughter is related to making and strengthening human connections. Laughter occurs when people are comfortable with one another when they feel open and free. And the more laughter there is, the more bonding occurs within the groups. This feedback "loop" of bonding-laughter-more bonding, combined with the common desire not to be singled out from the group, maybe another reason why laughter is often contagious.

Inaction in Crisis (Normalcy Bias)

Normalcy bias is a human strange reaction that makes people freeze. People become abnormally calm and pretend everything is normal in a crisis. It isn't true that people's fight-or-flight instincts kick in and they panic when disaster strikes. [McRaney 2011]

No matter what people encounter in life, their first analysis of any situation is to see it in the context of what is normal for them and then compare and contrast the new information against what they know usually happens. Because of this, people tend to interpret strange and alarming situations as if they were just part of business as usual.

The tendency to flounder in the face of danger is well understood and expected among tornado chasers and meteorologists. Weather experts and emergency management workers know you can become enveloped in a blanket of calm when terror enters your heart. Psychologists refer to it as normalcy bias. First responders call it negative panic. This strange counterproductive tendency to forget self-preservation in the event of an emergency is often factored into fatality predictions in everything from ship sinking to stadium evacuation. Disaster movies get it all wrong. When people are warned of danger, they don't evacuate immediately while screaming and flailing their arms.

About 75 percent of people find it impossible to reason during a catastrophic event or impending doom. On the edges, the 15 or so percent on either side of the bell curve react either with unimpaired, heightened awareness or blubbering, confused panic. The sort of people who survive is the sort of people who prepare for the worst and practice ahead of time. They've done the research, or built the shelter, or run the drills. They look for the exits and imagine what they will do. They were in a fire as a child or survived a typhoon. These people don't deliberate during calamity because they've already done the deliberation the other people around them are just now going through.

The brain must go through a procedure before the body acts – cognition, perception, comprehension, decision, implementation, and then movement. There's no way to overclock this, but people can practice until these steps individually are no longer complex, and thus no longer take up valuable brain computation cycles.

Normalcy bias isn't freezing at the first signs of danger like a rabbit who confronts a snake, which is a real behavior humans can succumb to. To suddenly stop moving and hope for the best is called fear bradycardia, and it is automatic and involuntarily instinct. This is sometimes referred to as tonic immobility.

<u>Excuses to Limit Failure</u> (Self-Handicapping)

Self-handicapping is another odd reaction making people cautious over possible outcomes. People often create conditions for failure ahead of time to protect their ego. It isn't true that in all people do, they strive for success. [McRaney 2011]

Chances are we know someone who seems to be in a perpetual state of illness. Maybe it's you, but let's assume it isn't. This person, the hypochondriac, is always complaining about a cold or a fever, a sick stomach or an aching back. For those who habitually see themselves as unwell, there are several benefits. A true hypochondriac absorbs empathy like a flower does sunshine, but the real reward comes when life gets too hard. When a project or an obligation seems like too much to handle, a hypochondriac can conveniently become sick and avoid the risk of failing.

From time to time a project will come along that seems so big and challenging people start to question their ability to succeed. It could be as epic as writing a book or directing a major motion picture, or it could be something more pedestrian like passing a final exam or delivering an important speech to the corporate boss. Naturally, some doubts will float through our minds whenever a failure is possible. Sometimes, when the fear of failure is strong, we use a technique psychologists call self-handicapping to change the course of our future emotional state. Self-handicapping is a real negotiation, an unconscious manipulation, of both our perceptions and those of others, that we use to protect our ego. Like its cousin's sour grapes, in which we pretend we don't want what we can't have, and sweet lemons, in which we convince ourselves something unpleasant is not so bad, self-handicapping is what psychologists call an anticipatory rationalization. Self-handicapping behaviors are investments in a future reality in which we can blame our failure on something other than our ability. If we succeed in an event, we can say we did so despite terrible odds. If we fall short, we can blame the events leading up to the failure instead of our incompetence or inadequacy.

<u>Pessimism Prevails</u> (Learned Helplessness)

Learned helplessness is a strange reaction making people accept bad situations. People tend to be pessimistic in front of difficult situations. They get used to hardship when it is intricate to achieve improvements. If people feel they are not in control of their destiny, they will give up and accept whatever situation they are in. It isn't true that it would be possible to think that it is normal for human beings to do whatever they can to escape a bad situation. [McRaney 2011]

Learned helplessness springs from all organisms' desire to conserve resources. If people cannot escape a source of stress, it leads to more stress, and this positive feedback loop eventually triggers an automatic shutdown. In extreme situations, people think if they keep struggling they may die, therefore, stopping gives them a chance the bad thing will go away.

If throughout life people have experienced crushing defeat or pummeling abuse, or loss of control, they convince themselves over time that there is no escape, and if escape is offered, people will not act – people become a nihilist who trusts futility instead of optimism.

When the average person fails, he or she will look for external forces to blame. Some people blame themselves and assume they are stupid. This is the explanatory style. People see events affecting their life along three gradients: personal, permanent, and pervasive. Pessimism and optimism are opposed to the extremes of the gradient. Pessimists often give up to defeat and stop trying. The more pessimistic the explanatory style, the easier it is for people to slip into learned helplessness.

When battered women, or hostages, or abused children, or longtime prisoners refuse to escape, they don't because they have accepted the futility of trying. What does it matter? Those who do get out of bad situations often have a hard time committing to anything that may lead to failure. It is well known that in nursing homes where conformity and passivity are encouraged, the health and well-being of patients decline rapidly. If instead, the people in these homes are given responsibilities and choices, they may remain healthy and active.

<u>Venting Increases Aggression</u> (Catharsis)

Catharsis is a strange reaction that shouldn't be expressed. Venting people's anger increases aggressive behavior over time. It isn't true that venting is an effective way to reduce stress and prevent lashing out at friends and family. [McRaney 2011]

Let it out is the motto of venting. Left inside us, the anger will fester and spread, grow like a tumor, boil up until we punch holes in the wall or slam our car door so hard the windows shatter. Those dark thoughts shouldn't be tamped down inside our hearts where they can condense and strengthen, where they form a concentrated stockpile of negativity that could reach critical mass at any moment.

Go get one of those squishy balls and work it over with death grips. Use both hands and choke the imaginary life out of it. Head to the gym and assault a punching bag. Shoot some people in a video game. Scream into a pillow. Feel better? Sure do. Venting feels great.

The problem is, it accomplishes little else. It makes matters worse and primes people's future behavior by fogging their minds.

If we think catharsis is good, we are more likely to seek it out when we get pissed. When we vent, we stay angry and are more likely to keep doing aggressive things so we can keep venting. It's druglike because there are brain chemicals and other behavioral reinforcements at work. If we get accustomed to blowing off steam, we become dependent on it. The more effective approach is to just stop. Take anger off of the stove.

<u>Overstimulation</u> (Supernormal Releasers)

Supernormal releasers are strange reactions people show on special occasions produced by overstimulation. Men can do things that look insane following their instincts, and women can marry men for interests beyond understanding. However, the truth is that in both cases supernormal releasers are the one which defines the outcomes men and women choose. [McRaney 2011]

This sort of behavior is common across the animal kingdom. Anything that directly affects our survival can become a superstimulus if exaggerated enough. If people associate something with survival but find an example of that thing that is more perfect than anything our ancestors could have ever dreamed of – it will overstimulate them.

When it comes to mate selection, the genders are usually divided into two camps. One has to carry the offspring and reproduce less often; the other can reproduce many times over without much risk. In this scenario, supernormal releasers either exaggerate the fertility and health of the egg carriers, or the status and resources of the sperm carriers.

For human ladies, a tux on a man who owns a private jet and three homes in Italy creates a powerful set of supernormal releasers. For human guys, symmetry, big breasts, wide hips, narrow waists, lustrous hair, and voluptuous lips add up to a powerful supernormal releaser. Most men wouldn't have sex with a plastic dolly, but the strength of plastic dolls sales over the years shows some will.

One crucial aspect which seems to be held above all others when men are making a snap judgment about physical attraction is the hip-to-waist ratio. In many studies around the world, no matter what cultural significance is placed on body type, a ratio in which the waist is about 70 percent the width of the hips is always preferred.

For women, a superstimulus has to have more than just a rocking body and a good hip-to-waist ratio. Women have more to lose when they make a bad decision, so they have evolved a more complex and particular set of metrics by which potential mates are judged. Those include, but are not limited to, economic capacity, social status, ambition, stability, intelligence, commitment, and height. Anyone of these guides for reproductive success in both a short-term or long-term mate can become a superstimulus, but for a man to be a supernormal releaser he would need to possess several of them.

Part IV: Evaluating Socialism

"Imagine no possessions," "No need for greed or hunger," "A brotherhood of man," "You may say I'm a dreamer," "But I'm not the only one." – John Lennon

To evaluate socialism the only thing we need is to understand this song. Dreams are good but the reality is harsh. Better be realists and progress from there, incorporate some dreams and discard others.

"In practice, socialism didn't work. But socialism could never have worked because it is based on false premises about human psychology and society, and gross ignorance of the human economy." -- David Horowitz

"Socialism is for those who think most people are losers. Capitalism is for those who think most people can take care of themselves." -- John Hawkins

It's easy to understand why people are emotionally drawn to the ideals of socialism, it is because it derives its fundamental motivational sources from human's compassionate instincts. In humans, compassion is always there, and so the socialist message abuses from human sensitivity twisting the purpose of compassion. We must give the devil his due, unfortunately, socialists use human weaknesses for their benefit.

According to socialists, the central concept of socialism is a visualization of human beings as social entities united by their common humanity. Socialists choose cooperation instead of competition and favor collectivism over individualism. Fundamentally, socialism favors the collective ownership of the means of production instead of the egoistic view promoting the private property.

According to some authors, socialism evolved as a reaction against the social and economic conditions produced in Europe by the growth of industrial capitalism. Therefore, socialism represents an economy where the workers own the means of production. This is to ensure that the class that produces the wealth of society collectively decides how it will be used for the benefit of all. Working unions were the firsts trying to implement socialism and their mission was to ensure equality among all employees and all management in the factory. Socialism was associated with the development of a new but growing class of industrial workers, who suffered the poverty and deprivation that were so often a feature of industrialization.

Socialists use to vent the importance of socialism, "In a socialist economy, there is great equality of income distribution as compared with a free market economy. A socialist economy is categorized by public ownership of the means of production and distribution. It is centrally planned and operates under the supervision of a central planning authority. It functions within definite objectives, such as aggregate demand, full employment, the satisfaction of communal demand, allocation of factors of production, distribution of the national income, the amount of capital accumulation, and economic development."

Socialists exaggerate their contribution to the population, "Production in state-owned industries is generally governed by the inclinations of consumers, and the available merchandises are distributed at fixed prices through the state-run department stores. The pricing process under socialism ideology does not operate freely but works under the control and regulation of the central planning authority."

Behavioral Evaluation

Evaluating socialism according to human nature generates many criticisms. Socialism claims a just society but it has never been implemented. Socialism enforces many regulations under an invented social justice but it never satisfies society. Socialism wants to promote the participation of all but does not understand the principle of division of labor that facilitates the organization of the economy. Socialism creates a society full of cheaters and slackers that do not collaborate with the ends of society.

Socialism is a backward based ideology because it perpetuates old views of the world without promoting constant knowledge. Socialists don't admit their ignorance and are not capable of improving according to their mistakes. Not because capitalism has not succeeded in eliminating poverty means it is not a valid approach. Socialism claims, without proof, it is more beneficial than capitalism, and it is well known that socialists have no valid criteria to measure its goodness. Human principles are not in the socialist agenda because socialism is opposed to human nature.

The Behavioral Framework of motivators, doing or acting, personal influences, social influences, and justifications, is a tool to organize the different concepts. Let us summarize the characteristics of socialism related to human nature using the framework.

Chapter 19: Motivations

The main motivators related to socialism include staying eternally in power, socialists are so deluded that they believe their approach is the unique solution to human difficulties. Socialism is a bad copy of communism which at least is sincere and pushes for the dictatorship of the proletariat, socialists hide their true intentions. The ideological background of socialism is based on the public ownership of the means of production, elimination of private property, elimination of the rich, total control of the state, and a misguided justice. Socialism is a non-humanistic approach because they don't understand humans, they just invented their view of a new human. Socialism borrows some ideas from religions, misinterpreting religious precepts. Socialists cheer up superstitions, making people believe in strange occurrences. Socialists are always blaming capitalism and the world functions in a real context of monetary transactions. Socialism proposes an approach absent from science, their beliefs are fanatical, not realists. Socialists fabricate heroes to run the country and benefit from people's weaknesses to control the population. Socialists are ignorant of evolution, humans have not evolved biologically for hundreds of thousands of years. Socialism is a fantasy-based approach that expects too much from humans. And socialism misses on diversity, they don't understand that humans are different and have individual inclinations.

Eternally in Power
- Socialists want to stay in power until their death, there is no way to convince them of their mistaken and wrongful approach. All socialist experiences have lasted several years, the Soviet Union, China, North Korea, Cuba, are examples.
- Socialists believe their approach has to be universal and they keep fighting around the world to impose their wrongful doctrine. This universality is one of the main concepts of socialism and communism.
- Socialists are not capable of consolidating a prosperous society and have decided to stay eternally trying. Staying longer in power does not guarantee success, the approach is non-viable.

Copying Communism
- Socialism, the stage before communism, follows the same approach of communism. It is an authoritarian type of regime that does not accept dissidence. The state is the authoritarian figure of socialism.
- Socialism is a state-based approach where people are just objects. The state controls the life of citizens. The state is a unique decision-maker. Al least communism foresees to eliminate the state.
- Socialism is a bad copy of communism. Socialism makes people believe in democracy but they prepare the grounds to stay eternally in power through authoritarianism.

Ideological Background
- Socialism is an old doctrine, it was suggested hundreds of years ago and the ideological bases are flawed.
- Socialism is not reality-based, the affect heuristic makes people believe socialism is possible independently of its failure.
- Socialism wants to change the unfair nature of the world without creating opportunities for all. On the contrary, some unmerited socialists get an opportunity and the rest get sidelined.
- Socialism is an assistance-oriented approach and not everybody needs help. Welfare must be well administered. There are ages for work and ages for assistance. There are health conditions for work and others for assistance.
- Socialism is an ego-oriented type of doctrine that only seeks to satisfy the vanity of the elite. In all the failed experiences of socialism, the elite is the one who lives well and prospers, the rest live worst.
- Socialists use logical fallacies to play with the needs of people providing goods and services at reduced prices. People apply wishful thinking and believe they are better off being subsided.
- Socialism proposes a survival-oriented society where productivity is not important. Socialists know how to eat the cake but they are incapable of making it.
- Socialists believe their duty, the universal appeal of socialism, is disconnected from the real needs of the population.
- In socialism, work is not important whereas loyalty to the state is a must.

- Socialism is not knowledge-driven. There is no possibility of improvement in a society that rejects research to improve life.
- Socialists are lousy at math, for example, they propose barter instead of monetary transactions.
- Socialists don't understand commerce and productivity, they are lousy on the economic basement of a society. Socialists don't know how to generate wealth and they believe things are free.
- Socialists consider humans manipulable, that anything can be done with them, that their human nature can be altered capriciously, for example, that people must be all equal.
- The free market is abolished because it is individually driven. Individuals have no independence to pursue their dreams.
- Socialism promotes a twisted system of rights and duties invented by bureaucrats without taking into consideration people. People suffer and there is no answer from socialists.
- Socialism is a doctrine without proof of validity, it manipulates the unconscious to make people act consciously in favor of socialism.
- Socialism does not deliver solutions, it increases the problems. Sorry for you socialists!

Misunderstood Equality
- Socialists are the firsts to claim equality. Today, nobody believes in the equality transmitted by socialists, it is a lie.
- It is a mistake to use the concept of equality erratically, diversity is too strong on humans.
- A simplistic meaning of equality does not solve the problems of humanity.

Non-Humanistic Approach
- Socialism makes people believe it is humanistic when in fact the authoritarian nature of its government demonstrates otherwise. Socialism does not improve the lives of people.
- Socialism goes against humanism because it promotes a biased approach oriented to crush the status quo and stay indefinitely in power. It is disrespectful of humans, science, and reasoning.

Religious Inspiration
- Socialists are influenced by religion, for example, they use egalitarianism, divine justice, and sacrifice on their favor and not to improve people's life.

- In socialism superstition is common. Socialists are prone to supernatural beliefs. Many socialists leaders have a pact with the devil.
- People believe socialist's charismatic leaders have supernatural powers.
- According to socialists, there are miraculous forces behind socialism, its supernatural justice is inevitable.
- Socialists have taken the worse supernatural suggestions into their doctrine. Socialism eternal appeal is inspired by god believers.
- In a society, not everybody is good, nor splendid, nor fair. Therefore, reward those who contribute and punish those who misbehave.

Cheering up Superstitions
- Socialists benefit from people's superstitions to maintain their doctrine alive.
- People's beliefs of a better society or human equality are manipulated by socialists.
- Some people believe in superstitious socialism and believe it is possible independently of its results.

Blaming Capitalism
- Socialists criticize capitalism as the generator of poverty, saying capitalism does not deliver good results. However, capitalism has been in power for centuries improving the lives of people.
- Socialists repeat critics to capitalism over and over, after so much repetition, people start believing it is true.
- Any political system wants to build a world just and fair, capitalism can perform, socialism has no way to demonstrate its viability.
- Capitalism gives priority to the creation of jobs and it can also assist the needy. Socialism fails to perform in both aspects.
- Socialism has no clear approach to productivity and it is against the prominence of the individual.
- Socialists create many prejudices against capitalism. Capitalism is always blamed as the cause of all people's troubles.
- Socialists use the anchoring effect to criticize capitalism, creating a false matrix of opinion at the base of their doctrine.

- Socialists will find out too late, that blood, sweat, and tears don't bring prosperity. People will change up their minds after so many failures.
- Critics of capitalism are welcomed but socialists fantasies are better kept on children's books and not in our society.

Absence of Science
- Socialism promotes a virtual reality impossible to attain, dismissing science and many other advanced disciplines.
- Socialism should rather learn from scientific studies describing the characteristics of human beings.
- Socialists despise social sciences because their doctrine is not based on science but fiction.
- Socialism is still around not because their doctrine is valid and viable, it is because people love to believe in myths, independently of its performance.
- Socialism and science are not compatible. Socialism is socially motivated rather than human nature, mathematical or economically motivated.
- Socialists avoid the scientific judgment of the consequences of their actions because they fail miserably.
- Socialism is a self-fulfilling prophecy because it is defined socially, not scientifically.
- Socialism needs to include science and admit its ignorance to recognize its weaknesses.
- Socialists don't promote progress, they prefer to live in the past, following a wrong routine, instead of looking for improvements.

Fabricating Heroes
- Socialists use to identify the greatest heroes of the past, such as independence or revolutions, to build an opinion matrix favoring the relationship between independence heroes and current heroes.
- Supporters get fascinated by the representation of their current hero, how similar he is to the ancient hero, the coincidences are astounding, miraculous.
- Some socialists leaders use to identify historic facts and use them for their benefits.
- People believe the leader has superpowers coming from the hero's grave.

- The hero's journey script fights for justice, he insults Imperialism or the United States and people love him.
- People love those who dare to confront the biggest forces in the world and socialism exploits that weakness.

Ignorance on Evolution
- Socialism has decided what the course of society must be and rejects the conventional wisdom that evolution has traced.
- Socialists don't understand biological evolution, they believe it is only cultural considerations that matter.
- The dilemma between human biological and cultural evolution is one of the main weaknesses of socialism.
- Socialism likes to be considerate towards the needy but twist its objectives to win adepts instead of doing good.
- In socialism, the family and the political order are disconnected. Socialism does not work for the benefit of families. It works for the benefit of the state.
- Socialists are excellent procrastinators, they keep assuring a better life for all but never attain their objective.
- Socialists use the bystander effect quite well, nobody complains because everybody thinks others would respond.

Fantasy-based Explanations
- Socialists stick to fantasy, therefore, they never will be able to lead a genuine transformation.
- Socialists know people are always inventing their life, therefore, politicians please people's desires of justice and equality in fantasy-land.
- People create their fiction of events to penalize democracy and support socialism. People are supporting a fantasy instead of a reality.
- In socialism, people accept a dubious doctrine as the panacea to solve all the problems of society. Of course, some people are at fault.
- Socialists are experts in making people accept and conform, the proof is that even under a socialistic created hunger, people don't complain.
- Socialists use to present the military forces on TV such that people understand that when force is needed, it will be put on the streets.

- Socialists tend to inflate the expectations of people to gain their support. Taking private property for the benefit of the poor, taking factories to be run by the workers, and so on.
- Many supporters of socialism are people who had no chances in life and consider socialism their salvation.
- Socialists cannot prove their system satisfies the population.

Missing on Diversity
- Socialism wants people to become someone else. Socialists try to change human beings to follow a unique invented model.
- If it is clear that people are different, why socialists have decided to make everybody equal?
- Socialists simplify things and come up with a handful of interpretations of life instead of recognizing the multiplicity of alternative life viewpoints.
- Socialists don't understand that each human is born with a fixed set of behavioral characteristics that are difficult, if not impossible, to change and that humans are all different.

Chapter 20: Actions

The main doing or acting characteristics are related to the use of language, socialists are manipulators of people through language. Regarding the management of groups, socialists are lousy defining groups, they don't understand the limitations of groups. Socialism has invented a new order but people are not buying the idea. Socialist's understanding of happiness and misery is very poor, the doctrine leads rather to suffering. The implementation of the authoritarian state is the main objective of socialism, imposing a unique view from the top of the hierarchy. Socialists manipulate the poor on their benefit, control them, and stay in power. Socialists exploit obedience, they know people are obedient and patient even under harsh conditions. Socialists accept the suffering of the population provided the elite keeps eternal power. Socialism implements gossip as a tool to control the population. Socialism plans for boredom, it is a cheating and slacking approach built from the top. Socialists use laughter to make believe the population is happy. Socialists suffer from inaction in crisis, they know things are not well but they keep doing business as usual. And socialists convince people to accept suffering in the name of a better society, that would be built a hundred years from now.

Language as a Weapon
- Socialism uses language to perpetuate their fiction of a better society. Socialists use metaphors to manipulate their partisans.
- Words and schemes are routinely used to convince partisans of their adequacy. Although in practice nothing improves.
- It is common to hear words such as Imperialism, exploitation, injustice, used to gain the support of the population.

Grouping's Misconception
- Socialists feel protected within their group and don't accept outsiders. Only those that follow the pack are welcomed, the rest is penalized with ostracism and discrimination.
- Socialists excel at group thinking; when the leaders are around, partisans obey the orders without complaining.
- Socialists recommend unproductive decisions making in groups letting the whole group come up with solutions, invoking a fictive need of participation. Socialists don't understand organization principles.

- Socialists are penalized by inefficiency because their doctrine promotes the participation of people without qualifications.
- In socialism, the leader meets with thousands of partisans and transmit his orders; the group has to obey, there is no discussion, the decisions have already been made.

Socialists' Failed New Order
- Socialists have invented their new order and plan to impose it on the rest of the population.
- Socialists want to destroy the old order and construct a new one; however, their new order is not viable, therefore, people are going to pay the consequences.
- Because socialism is a myth, socialists must safeguard their status quo by any means, violence and coercion are normal approaches.
- Are there true believers of socialism? Of course, socialism cannot be sustained by violence only. What happens is that socialists are blinded by their ideals and don't want to admit defeat.
- Socialists use unjust discrimination and sectarianism; those that differ from them are penalized by current institutional administrators.

Forgetting Socialists Mistakes
- In socialism people are busy solving daily problems, they forget about the lack of democracy, and the politicians and entrepreneurs keep stealing the country's treasure.
- Socialists are good magicians, they know how to fool their partisans, they create stories of wars with neighboring countries to make people forget about the difficulties of daily life.
- Socialists live in chaos but they believe they have control over their surroundings. Electricity, water, food, and propane distribution are chaotic but they feel in control of all the factors.
- Socialists are limited in their view of the world and cannot understand its complexity. A society needs funds for public and private projects, socialists don't understand this.

The Totalitarian State
- The socialist state is in charge of all the responsibilities, including misinterpreting the context and the definition of people's duties.
- The socialist state promotes unjust equality, limiting the freedom of individuals and the free enterprise.

- Socialists take for granted that they have to eliminate private property and decide what the consumers need.
- The state controls everything, people's work, where they live, what they eat, how many hours they sleep and study.

Imposing Social Acceptance
- Socialists know that social acceptance is natural and people don't want to contradict the imagined majority.
- People are bombarded with socialist propaganda and they believe there is a majority supporting the system.
- Socialists know very well that people conform, and exploit that weakness on their benefit.

Manipulating The Poor
- Socialists choose partisans coming from the poor and promote them to important posts, just to demonstrate how good they are.
- For example, a military coming from the poor or a bus driver taking the presidency.
- The unproductive poor knows he has no future in a wealth-based society, therefore, he leans toward welfare-based socialism that does not promote productivity.

Exploiting Obedience
- Socialists benefit from obedient citizens that have no critical thinking.
- Individuals are not important in the socialists' approach, only obedience is important for socialists.
- Obedient citizens are born to take care of their children, work, eat, sleep, and enjoy but are incapable of challenging the state.
- Socialists' obedient partisans have not improved the life of the population. All socialist's experiences have had an obedient population at their disposal and nothing good happened.
- What is needed is smart people disposed to challenge the proposals constructively. Socialists must yield to knowledge-based arguments.

Implementing Gossip
- Socialists use gossip profusely, it is a bonding behavior that makes people talk more than expected.
- Socialists talk about the opposition and invent stories to blame them for all miseries.

- Socialists design gossip structures in the community to detect defectors. The well known CDR in Cuba has controlled the population for many years.
- Socialist gossip is so strong that in many cases socialists can be overthrown because of their invented gossip structure.

Planning for Boredom
- Socialists are the masters of boredom, they despise work. Socialists don't understand research, one of the tools to improve a society.
- Socialists plan for boredom, they design their policies to make people yawn irremediably. Many socialists spend hours on line to buy basic foods or medicines.
- It is not that boredom is psychological, it is that socialists make, on purpose, an environment favorable to cheating, slacking, and procrastination.

Using Laughter
- Socialists use laughter while they are with their partisans, promoting bonding and subordination. In many cases that laughter is hypocritical.
- Socialists laugh at the opposition and make fun of them, rejecting its petitions of a better society. Socialists satirize the opposition violating their rights.

Inaction in Crisis
- Socialists are specialists in keeping inaction in crisis, they don't move a finger during harsh epochs.
- Socialists are a disaster and they keep calm as if nothing is happening.
- Socialists live in normalcy bias mode all their life because they are unable to recognize the difference between normal and abnormal.
- Socialists have a severe misunderstanding of what a functional society is and are incapable of solving the problems of society.

Convincing People
- Socialists use to convince partisans to join their cause offering gratuities, and cheap food, imported medicines from communist countries, houses taken from the rich and devalued services.
- Socialists know people feel overstimulation when things are free.
- Socialism requires people's productivity and it is well known that many socialists don't contribute their share.

- Socialists create an illusory doctrine to attract people, hiding reality under the umbrella of a fictive social justice.
- Socialists have bombarded the minds of the population for years, telling them how good things will be in socialism. It never happens.
- Even if things don't improve in socialism, people are primed by the belief in a better future and they don't recognize the system's failure.
- People in socialism keep waiting for a good life, it may take them the whole life.
- Socialism's biased social justice and rationale are still believed by some people. They are stubborn partisans.
- Socialism makes people believe that they are helping consolidate a better society different than any existing one. The unattainable dream that never comes true.

Chapter 21: Personal Factors

Among the personal characteristics, socialists exploit emotions, they are the masters of psychology and psychiatry. Socialists exploit the current and remembering self to make partisans believe they are correct. Socialists hire liars to cheat and express their happiness with the system. Socialism promotes envy and people express their discontentment blaming the rich. Socialists vent their anger, producing a spiral effect that keeps growing over time. Socialists suspect individual positions, they don't appreciate original solutions coming from individuals. Socialists try to hide reality from the population and blame others for their fault. Socialists argue from ignorance and have no clear view of what is needed to run society. Socialists benefit from people's weaknesses and stay in power under the worst circumstances. Socialists create important people archetypes such that the population does not complain. Socialists attack the person instead of the idea. Socialists have trust and truth confusion and prefer their loyal partisans instead of productive people. And socialism is a pessimistic approach because it allows general suffering on the population without remorse.

Exploiting Emotions
- Socialists are experts in psychology and probably on psychiatry. On human emotions, they excel, for the benefit of the elite.
- Socialists have specialists studying the weaknesses of human beings and use that knowledge to subdue the population.
- Socialists manage emotions very well and they know people are susceptible to manipulation. People want to believe in a better society and succumb to the approach.
- Socialists engage in the eternal fight of egalitarianism or of poor against the rich or the inconvenience of capitalism.
- People are primed on the hopeful emotional ideas of a new society and they reject the failure of the socialist approach.
- The majority in many cases is poor, therefore, they feel emotions of envy and believe that economic equality is a good objective for a society.
- People are lousy at logic and are filled up with impractical, emotional, socialist beliefs.

- Socialism exploits emotions and promises unattainable paradises, people cannot assimilate that knowledge on time, and it takes time to understand the non-viability of socialism.
- On the long list of human emotions, socialists would find arguments to twist each human emotion toward their socialist fictional objective.
- Socialists use the affect heuristic to convince partisans. People overestimate the rewards of socialism and only when the harsh reality shows up they are finally punished after recognizing their mistake.

Manipulating Current and Remembering Self
- When not in power, socialists use the conflict between the current and remembering self to convince their supporters that the experience in capitalism has been awful.
- When in power, they fail, and people's current self shouldn't forget socialist failures either.
- Countries that suffered socialism don't repeat the mistake. But countries which didn't suffer socialism are the targets of such a flawed doctrine.
- Socialism should never be tried.

Hiring Liars
- Socialists are experts hiring people to lie about their life difficulties. It is a propaganda machine.
- When socialism fails to provide services such as domestic propane, electricity, water, socialists find people to lie saying they receive the service regularly, and that the services are excellent.

Promoting Envy
- Socialism tends to choose the worst emotions of indignation, resentment, and envy to guide its partisans. Envy is very strong in the poor population and socialists know it.
- Socialist's fight against private property is a clear example of envy utilized to convince their partisans. Most partisans don't care if they steal the houses of other people.

Venting Anger
- Socialists leaders are always venting their anger. The people are always subject to a violent message.
- Socialists leaders make people believe they are doing a great job and they vent the anger over the opposition.

- Socialists leaders' anger creates a resentful population, ready to hit their neighbors in the future.

Suspecting Individuals
- Socialism is suspicious of individual preferences because they use to go against the desires of the socialist state.
- Because socialism is an authoritarian doctrine, it cannot accept an individual's subjective expectations. For socialists, the objective conditions are set at the outset by the state.
- Socialists are suspicious of feelings and preferences of ordinary people because they contradict socialists principles, such as equality, private property or collectivization.

Manipulating Happiness and Misery
- Socialists manipulate the happiness and misery characteristics of people to maintain a submissive society that accepts the socialist disaster without protesting.
- People in socialism get used to the dramatic miserable situation balancing their happiness ups and downs.
- Socialists don't talk about happiness, they don't propose any measurement or yardstick, happiness is not on their agenda.
- Socialism proposes a unique view of well-being, the "socialist's well-being." Follow the commandments of the socialist state instead of the individual's instincts.
- Socialists impose biased yardsticks for goodness and beauty and the socialist state is in charge of defining them.
- Happiness is an individual feeling, therefore, socialism is incapable of understanding why people feel discontentment.
- Socialists are against the capitalistic view of happiness, for them the free market is a sin.
- Socialists promote alcoholism and drug abuse to maintain individuals distracted by the socialist's disaster.
- Socialists benefit from the Buddhist's "within one's body insight" (instead of the outside world) because they manipulate people's emotions to stay in power.
- Socialists are happy with the Buddhist approach because people stop craving for a better life and accept whatever they get to survive.

Arguing from Ignorance
- People's ignorance makes them accept the possibility of socialism because they don't have enough arguments to prove otherwise. They have not had socialism before, they wait to see.
- People accept socialism because they have doubts about socialism and they don't understand the doctrine, they argue from ignorance.
- Socialism is an alternative that sounds great as a dream but has no practical support.
- Socialists use cognitive bias on their benefit and ask the people to be patient, that in one hundred years or more they are going to find paradise. And people believe them because they have illusions.

Benefiting from Weaknesses
- Socialists play with the weaknesses of people, the people are the message, and for them, the leader is the messenger.
- Beware, socialists use to exploit people's weaknesses in their benefit and not on people's future.
- Socialism uses the center of attention weakness in two distinct ways; when looking for power and once in power.
- When looking for power, socialists exploit the center of attention by pushing individuals to show non-conformity with the status quo.
- Once in power, socialists prompt people to shift their center of attention towards unjust suffering for the good of all.
- When socialists take power, they use the spotlight effect to guarantee nobody is complaining about the government.
- People are more scared of socialism than in democracy. Fear is too strong in socialism because socialists manipulate survival instincts.
- In socialism, people know they are scrutinized by the state and they are scared of losing their privileges, such as cheaper food and subsided services.

Important People Archetypes
- Socialists are specialists in creating the important people's atmosphere to control the majority of the population.
- Socialists leaders use to be charismatic or originating from the military or other powerful institutions such as the church.
- Socialists also create the archetypes of the rich, the savior, the knowledgeable, the smart as the monsters of capitalism or Imperialism.

- A representativeness heuristic is a powerful tool exploited by socialism to humiliate people. People in socialism have to succumb to authority.
- Socialists believe their opinions and decisions are based on experience and facts, while those who disagree with them are falling for the lies and propaganda of sources people shouldn't trust.
- Socialists are always right, the rest of us are deluded.

Attacking the Person
- Socialists attack the person representing the opposition instead of the ideas being expressed.
- Socialists use to criticize others saying that they are deluded, that they are not getting the facts.
- Socialists use the ad hominem fallacy against their opponents. They attack always the person because they don't have arguments to defend socialism.

Confusing Truth and Trust
- Socialists are so mistaken in their judgment that trust and truth are mixed up.
- For socialists, loyalty is fundamental, they want obedient people whom they can trust and at the same time, they want these supporters to be truthful.
- Anybody not loyal to the socialist cause is considered an enemy.
- Opponents caught in the untruthful current are always going to be penalized.

Pessimistic Approach
- In socialism, people demonstrate pessimistic behavior because life is so harsh that they become sad.
- People give up the fight and accept the socialist regime because they don't see a way out.

Chapter 21: Social Factors

Among the social influences considered, socialism promotes cooperation, which by itself is a good feature, but at the cost of the freedom of the individual. Socialism promotes collectivization without understanding what are the limits of people working in groups. All socialists' regimes have canceled collectivization because is an awkward approach that does not produce results. Socialists are against human rights, they don't respect most rights on the name of maintaining their doctrine. Socialists use a strategy of lies to keep the population ignorant of what is going on. Socialism is evil because it goes against the population, the most penalized are the opposition. Socialists use vague statements to manipulate the population. Socialists believe they are highly gifted, that they are the smartest, and control the population and its surroundings. Socialists have so much inexperience because they have never run a society under such an approach. And socialism shows a lack of context, its doctrine was conceived hundreds of years ago and has not been updated to adapt to modern times. Socialism does not analyze the situation according to the world's reality and fails to produce good results.

Cooperation
- Socialists fail regarding cooperation because they think the organization of society is through a tribal one on one form of cooperation, instead of clusters of people cooperating with other clusters.
- Socialists don't understand evolution and believe cooperation is something built up into our human genetic code.
- Today, people are still living in small bands of dozen of individuals collaborating indirectly with the rest of society. The family is the most common cluster of collaboration. Socialism despises the family in favor of the state.
- Humans are always imagining their life in better conditions, a just society, fairness, and so on. Socialism benefits from such human weaknesses to keep people's hope alive.
- Socialists don't benefit the population because their doctrine is based on an imaginative homogeneous society that does not please everybody. Diversity is the champion in society.

Collectivization
- Socialists have twisted the order of priorities humans have to go through by imposing the collective viewpoint against such of the free individual.
- Collectivization has limitations, and it is clear that it is against nature. Human motivation is one of the greatest weaknesses of collectivization.
- Socialists insist on collectivization. Cuba, China, and the Soviet Union are clear examples of failed collectivization.
- Socialists don't understand what are the advantages and disadvantages of working in groups.
- Socialists believe in the creation of homogeneous groups capable of solving all the problems of society and it is well known that people are heterogeneous. Diversity is fundamental to improve the performance of groups.
- Socialists groups have many disadvantages, for example, group conformity to maintain harmony.
- Socialists form groups where the opposition is not welcomed, according to them dissent leads to chaos.

Human Rights Violations
- Socialism violates several human rights. Civil rights, economic rights, political rights, are constantly being violated.
- The socialist doctrine goes against human rights. Egalitarianism is a clear example of a violation of an individual's freedom.
- Liberty, equality before the law, and private property are not available in socialist countries.
- Socialists have too many difficulties with human rights, they are not able to guarantee the rights of the population.

Strategy of Lies
- Socialists benefit from people's limitations by bombarding the population with lies and retelling the lies over and over.
- In a socialists society, people tend to concentrate on survival and forget about any other source of discontentment, they are lying to themselves.
- When the socialist regime is incapable of providing basic services such as water, electricity, and propane, people forget about its authoritarian nature and stay a minute after minute trying to solve

- their shortages. People are caught in an eternal loop of invented lies.
- People lie and socialists lie to everybody but primarily to themselves.
- Their approach is a lie invented to make believe they are going to solve the problems of the world.
- Of course, the socialist leadership is always lying to the population.
- When socialists are in power things don't go well, therefore, they must lie to explain their failure.

Socialism is Evil
- Socialism belongs to the evil's category, it is worse than bad, it is the negation of humanity.
- Socialists have robbed the population of their idiosyncrasy.
- Socialists change the mode of behavior or way of thought peculiar to individuals, imposing a fictive communal approach.

Using Vague Statements
- Socialists are specialists in vague statements, "be patient, we are working for you."
- People need answers now, while they are alive, and not in the future, just for purposes of benefiting their descendants.

Praising Highly Gifted Socialists
- Socialists are the worse estimators of their incompetence and the difficulty of complex tasks.
- Socialists were not born to contribute to society, their doctrine is mentally flawed.
- "The stupids are cocksure while the intelligent are full of doubts." Socialists belong to the cocksure class of people.
- Most socialist leaders are cocksure while the opposition leaders are full of doubts.
- Socialist leaders are champions of offering miraculous solutions; however, all these solutions end without results and the situation gets worse than before.

Socialist Inexperience
- Socialists are characterized by not having the experience, there has not been a socialist society yet.
- It is not strange that socialists fail so miserably, the theory does not work.

- Most socialists leaders have demonstrated their ignorance after just a few months in power.
- When people hear the leader's speech they are convinced there is confidence in the future. What people don't know yet is that the leader is more ignorant than knowledgeable.

Lack of Context
- Socialists have a problem with the context in decision making, they don't consider the settings at all.
- Socialists know they live in a capitalistic world and nonetheless, they try to crush it, instead of building on top of it.
- If socialists had a better context-oriented type of judgment, they would try to blend their doctrine into a complementary type of capitalistic-socialistic approach.
- Socialists fail miserably on the analysis of the context, they cannot change the world just by blowing off capitalism.

Chapter 22: Rationale

Among the justification characteristics of socialism, hiding its results and statistics, they don't publish how are they doing. Socialists use the third party effect to invent explanations for their unpopular measures. Socialists have misunderstood equality and they are punished by their doctrine. Socialism is despotic, it is only its view that counts, it does not change direction under adversity. Socialism blames others, the fault is not the doctrine or the socialists but the others. Socialists are excellent at first impressions, what they lack is a sustained successful approach. Socialism has a lack of risk and benefits to sustain their doctrine. Socialists punish the opposition or their partisans and they punish them severely. Socialism is not success-oriented, there are no examples of socialism improving the lives of the population. Socialists require honesty, their approach is faulty, therefore, they must try to improve listening to non-socialists. Socialists explain failures pointing to others, to convince partisans that socialism is possible. Socialists are the best critics of the opposition and blame them for their unsuccessful approach. Socialists are incapable to perform, there is no way for them to succeed. The opposition to socialism must be active, a wrongful approach must not be allowed, socialism is faulty, it must be rejected, it is a flawed approach.

Hiding Results
- Socialists know pretty well they are not doing a good job. They don't provide statistics to hide their failure.
- Socialists never present proof of their performance.
- Socialists don't like First World standards to be known by their supporters.
- Socialists have no yardstick to measure their misery.
- Socialists will never present statistics of failed socialist's experiences.
- Socialists use the confirmation bias repeating over and over that the failed experience was not a real socialist system, that they are building socialism over hundreds of years.

Hiding Reality
- Socialists exploit the inconsistency weakness of people. People in socialism wish to keep consistent over time (to have a future), independently of the harsh times.

- People want to believe that they have not changed their life whilst in socialism, however, their reality is so harsh that it is impossible to lie to themselves.
- When socialists receive new information that threatens their self-image, they react quickly to reaffirm their identity; they start blaming imperialistic or capitalistic forces.

Third-Party Effect
- For socialists, the third party is The People, every opinion against the regime is an attack to The People and it cannot be accepted; jail and punishment, if not dead are the consequences.
- Socialists avoid communicating the opposition's message to the population.
- The third-person effect is a version of the self-serving bias. Socialists excuse their failures and see themselves as more successful, more intelligent, and more skilled than others are.
- A good definition of a socialist is that they think they are right and their approach is invulnerable.

Despotic Socialism
- By definition socialism is despotic, therefore, it represents a despotic government.
- Socialism does not consider diversity and it is always ready to limit the freedoms of people in the name of the stability of the government.

Blaming the Victim
- Many socialists leaders use to praise the perpetrators of crimes, like in the cases of robbers or murderers, saying that the society was responsible for their misbehavior or they were poor.
- Justice, it is well known, recommends that the blame must always be on the perpetrator and not on the victim. The victim, of course, is always the population and the perpetrator is the state.

First Impressions
- Socialists know that on first impression their doctrine is attractive and can overshadow other political systems such as capitalism.
- "Socialism is for the good of the many, capitalism is for the good of the few," it's a common socialist point of view.
- Socialist partisans remain with their first impression and it takes time and harsh conditions to understand the mistake.

Misunderstanding Risks and Benefits
- Socialists play with risks and benefits, presenting a future full of benefits and no risks.
- Socialists don't understand the difficulties of life, they forget the risks, they only concentrate on supposed benefits.
- The risks of a socialists society have never been studied seriously by economists. If it had been done, most people would abhor socialism.

Punishing Failure
- Socialist leaders use to explain their failure by manipulating people's contributions on their behalf. Socialists identify the few cases of successful sports champions and take up their merits in the name of socialism.
- Socialist leaders accept partial responsibility but blame some of their partisans and in some cases punish them severely.

Few Successes
- Socialists use to present their friends' specific stories of success as representing the overall reality; giving free houses to a few partisans or selling goods and services at cheaper prices and publishing them in the news.
- The fact is that the majority is not getting a benefit, people are worse than ever but the socialist's media presents a distorted view of reality.
- Socialists always say that there is no example yet of socialism, that any experience going on in the world is just a simulation or a prototype of a socialist society.
- Because they don't know what are they looking for, they have no choice but to blame their failures on a misinterpretation of the real socialistic approach.
- When socialism gets in power, it takes just a few months to demonstrate that it is not viable.
- People in socialism must collaborate to allow change since socialism is not going to solve the population crises.

Socialist's Required Honesty
- Socialists should demonstrate the validity of their doctrine, check up its theory and update their approach.
- First, check the approach on a trial basis and demonstrate it works; make the corrections to adapt to the realities of the world.

- Socialism should pay attention to these remarks and start rebuilding their approach such that the population gets a real benefit.
- Just by promising a better future and never attaining it, socialism is doom, even the most fervent supporters are going to dismiss socialism as inadequate.

Explaining Failures
- Socialism is still an option because there are real examples, even though they are failed, still in power, such as the Soviet Union, China, Cuba, Venezuela.
- Socialists find several reasons to explain why these systems have failed. Of course, socialists don't accept failure.
- Socialism is incorrect, it is popular only because capitalism has not been able to solve all the problems.
- Socialists are experts finding explanations for their failure and they change the story every day to keep the population misinformed.
- Because of normal human limitations, people forget about what was going on just a few months ago.
- Socialists keep offering paradise on earth and part of the population believes it.

Critics to the Opposition
- Socialists use to criticize the opposition or the Empire but they never criticize themselves or their failures.
- Socialists are always ready to blame the opposition on supposed actions charging them of the lack of performance of the socialist approach.
- For socialists the opposition just wants to get rid of the socialist movement, the opposition becomes their enemy.
- If socialists had the possibility, they would be ready to exterminate their enemies.

Socialist Incapacity
- Socialists are not interested in accepting their inability to perform.
- Even in front of evidence, they tend to distort the facts on their behalf.
- Socialists are deluded on their aspirations to build a better society.
- Socialists cannot be honest, they don't recognize their faults and weaknesses.

- Socialists don't want to feel incompetent when getting in power, therefore, they invent stories and devise alternatives without theoretical or practical support.
- Socialists are a bunch of improvisers, and worst of all, they are not smart, they keep repeating the same mistakes over and over.
- Socialists have known for centuries their incapacity to succeed but they pretend their doctrine is positive and keep trying to convince people.
- Socialists have no choice but to fail when they get in power, therefore, they look for excuses all the time; Imperialism and capitalism are the main excuses.

Opposing Socialism
- The opposition has always signaled the socialist mistakes and blames the socialist system.
- People who have suffered socialism cannot accept the socialist approach.
- Socialists don't make any amends and keep going full throttle ahead without remorse. The opposition must do the same against the regime.
- Socialists should accept failure and rescind power. To manage a society, an open mind is required to solve the difficulties, socialists are 'square heads' that cannot understand the complexities of the world.
- In socialism, individuals must break apart from the pack and start fighting against it, if they don't do it, nobody would do.
- When people feel the socialist government is not delivering, they have the responsibility of expressing their disgust and they must protest against the regime.
- Not because the socialist regime is the authority people have to accept blindly their commands.
- Deep down in their minds, socialists know it is impossible to build socialism, predefined justice does not exist.
- I wish socialists in power were smarter and recognize their failure so that people had a chance to start over under a better approach.
- All the experiences related to socialism have been failures, there is no choice.

Bibliography

[Boloix 2017] Germinal Boloix, "Socialist Bingo: Knowledge Distorted Knowledge," Germinal Boloix Editor, 2017.

[Boloix 2018] Germinal Boloix, "Socialism is Dead, Nietzsche is Eternal," Germinal Boloix Editor, 2018.

[Boloix 2019] Germinal Boloix, "Socialism and Failed States," Germinal Boloix Editor, 2019.

[Brown 2009] Archie Brown, "The Rise and Fall of Communism," Doubleday Canada, 2009.

[Bueno 2011] Bruce Bueno de Mesquita, Alastair Smith, "The Dictator's Handbook, Why bad behavior is almost always good politics," PublicAffairs, Perseus Book Group, 2011.

[Chapko 2010] Bill Chapko, Nietzsche's best writings, Bill Chapko Editor. Internet version, 2010.

[Fleming 2008] Thomas Fleming, "Socialism," Marshall Cavendish Corporation, 2008.

[Gaona 2018] Jose Mauricio Gaona, "Democratic Blending: The New Model of Dictatorships in Latin America," Journal of International Affairs, June 12, 2018.

[Harari 2014] Yuval Noah Harari, "Sapiens, A Brief History of Humankind," McClelland & Stewart, 2014.

[Hayek 1994] F. A. Hayek, "The Road to Serfdom," The University of Chicago Press, Chicago 1994.

[Huenemann 2009] Charlie Huenemann, "Nietzsche: Genius of the Heart," Talking Donkey Press, 2009.

[Maslow 1970] Abraham Maslow, "Motivation and Personality," 2nd. ed., Harper & Row, New York, 1970.

[Merino 2010] Noel Merino, Book Editor, "Capitalism, Current Controversies," Greenhaven Press, 2010.

[McRaney 2011] David McRaney, "You are Not so Smart," Penguin Books Ltd. 2011.

[Nietzsche 1998] Friedrich Nietzsche, "Twilight of the Idols," Oxford University Press, 1998.

[Nietzsche 2003] Friedrich Nietzsche, "Thus Spoke Zarathustra," Penguin Books Ltd. (1961, 1969) 2003.

[Safranski 2002] Rudiger Safranski – Nietzsche, A Philosophical Biography, translated by Shelley Frish, W. W. Norton & Company, Inc. 2002.

[Scruton 2017] Roger Scruton, "On Human Nature," Princeton University Press, 2017.

[Steele 2017] Graham Steele, "The Effective Citizen," Nimbus Publishing Limited, 2017.

[Wilson 1978] Edward O. Wilson, "On Human Nature," Bantam New Age Books, 1978.

Epilogue

"Imagine no possessions," "A brotherhood of man," "I wonder if you can," "Imagine all the people," "Sharing all the world," aha-ah ah ah ah – John Lennon.

This song describes what many socialists dream for the future, the same dream Christians have had for centuries. It is an unattainable dream. Better stick to a less perfect world where some people have possessions and others don't. Where some groups are like brothers and other groups are not. Where some groups share the world and others don't. Maybe John Lennon didn't realize he was writing a song orientated to the socialist dream. The song is nice but the socialist political system is not, too many people are suffering because of Absurd Socialism, it is not acceptable.

Venezuela is still in limbo, the country has no chance of recovering while Absurd Socialism is in power. Something fishy is going on in the country, something is murky, why there is no response to a general claim for change? Unfortunately, Venezuelans have not reacted as expected and Absurd Socialism hangs on for an undefined period in power.

The year 2019 is passing by without results. Maduro was supposed to rescind power and it is still there. It is clear that Absurd Socialism still pulls the strings in Venezuela. Incredibly, a country has been kidnapped in such a miserable way. Those in power are responsible. All public administrators, employees, the military, and a group of the opposition that have allowed all this disaster to happen are at fault. Are they going to be punished in the future? That is what they deserve. I hope there is no amnesty for the main performers of such a cataclysm in Venezuela.

Are new elections going to be accepted by all the parties? Is the electoral system going to be updated? Without an up to date electoral listing where all voters are identified by the electoral center, it is impossible to guarantee a fair election. Each electoral center must be formed by members of all the parties to guarantee minimal supervision of the electoral results for each center. Let us hope there is a change of government that demonstrates an open mind for the benefit of all. The experience of Absurd Socialism has been a catastrophe and Venezuela does not deserve such a repulsive style of the political system.

www.ingramcontent.com/pod-product-compliance
Lightning Source LLC
Chambersburg PA
CBHW051757040426
42446CB00007B/402